THIS BOOK IS NO LONGER THE PROPERTY OF
THE UNIVERSITY OF CHICAGO LIBRARY

NATIONAL FOUNDATION FOR EDUCATIONAL
RESEARCH IN ENGLAND AND WALES
OCCASIONAL PUBLICATION SERIES

The i.t.a. Symposium

The
i.t.a. Symposium

Research Report on the
British Experiment with i.t.a.
by John Downing

Evaluations on the Report by
A. Sterl Artley, Sir Cyril Burt, Hunter Diack,
R. Gulliford, James Hemming, Jack A. Holmes,
A. R. MacKinnon, A. H. Morgan and M. Procter,
Marie D. Neale, Jessie F. Reid, M. D. Vernon

Introduction: H. L. Elvin   Summary: W. D. Wall

NATIONAL FOUNDATION FOR EDUCATIONAL RESEARCH
in England and Wales
THE MERE, UPTON PARK, SLOUGH, BUCKS

*Published by the National Foundation for Educational Research
in England and Wales*

*The Mere, Upton Park, Slough, Bucks
and at 79 Wimpole Street, London, W.1*

First Published 1967

© *National Foundation for Educational Research
in England and Wales, 1967*

LB1028
.N354
v. 15
cop. 2

Printed in Great Britain by
KING, THORNE & STACE LTD., SCHOOL ROAD, HOVE, SUSSEX

Contents

	page
LIST OF TABLES	v
LIST OF GRAPHS	vii
INTRODUCTION. H. L. ELVIN	ix

RESEARCH REPORT ON THE BRITISH EXPERIMENT WITH i.t.a. JOHN DOWNING

Chapter I. Historical Background and Origins of the i.t.a. Research ... 1

Chapter II. The First i.t.a. Experiment—Aims, Methodology and Design ... 3
1. Aims of the First i.t.a. Experiment. 2. Methodology of the First i.t.a. Experiment. 3. Design of the First i.t.a. Experiment. 4. Populations in the Initial Experiment. 5. Matching of Experimental with Control Groups. 6. Materials. 7. The Teachers and their Methods. 8. Procedure.

Chapter III. Results of the First i.t.a. Experiment ... 25
1. General Results related to Hypotheses. 2. Results for Low Achieving, Average Achieving, and High Achieving Segments of the Experimental and Control Groups. 3. Results of Check on Effectiveness of Attempts to Stimulate Hawthorne Effect in the Control Group.

Chapter IV. Conclusions ... 48

Contents

	page
TABLES E1-E29	56
GRAPHS 1-36	73
THE HISTORICAL BACKGROUND TO THE i.t.a. RESEARCH REPORT: A SELECTED BIBLIOGRAPHY	91

EVALUATIONS

1.	A. STERL ARTLEY	97
2.	SIR CYRIL BURT	100
3.	HUNTER DIACK	109
4.	R. GULLIFORD	112
5.	JAMES HEMMING	118
6.	JACK A. HOLMES	123
7.	A. R. MACKINNON	128
8.	A. H. MORGAN AND M. PROCTER	132
9.	MARIE D. NEALE	139
10.	JESSIE F. REID	148
11.	M. D. VERNON	155

THE EVALUATIONS: A SUMMARY. W. D. WALL	162

List of Tables

		page
1.	Number of Schools and Classes in First i.t.a. Experiment	9
2.	Maximum number of Experimental and Control Subjects in Matched Groups possible from the Matched Schools or Classes in the present Analysis of Data from the First i.t.a. Experiment	10
E1.	Progress in Reading Basic Reader Series	56
E2.	Results for Schonell Graded Word Reading Test given after 1 year and after $1\frac{1}{3}$ years in i.t.a. to i.t.a. group and in t.o. to t.o. group	57
E3.	Reading in i.t.a. versus Reading in t.o.—Accuracy	57
E4.	Reading in i.t.a. versus Reading in t.o.—Speed	58
E5.	Reading in i.t.a. versus Reading in t.o.—Comprehension	58
E6.	Transfer of Learning from i.t.a. to t.o.—Accuracy	59
E7.	Transfer of Learning from i.t.a. to t.o.—Speed	59
E8.	Transfer of Learning from i.t.a. to t.o.—Comprehension	60
E9.	Transfer of Learning from i.t.a. to t.o. in Experimental Group Pupils—Accuracy	60
E.10	Transfer of Learning from i.t.a. to t.o. in Experimental Group Pupils—Speed	61
E11.	Transfer of Learning from i.t.a. to t.o. in Experimental Group Pupils—Comprehension	61
E12.	Transfer of Learning from i.t.a. to t.o.—Word Recognition	62
E13.	Transfer of Learning from i.t.a. to t.o. in Experimental Group—Word Recognition	62

List of Tables

page

E14. Analysis of Errors Made in the t.o. Edition of Schonell's Graded Word Reading Test by 135 Experimental Group Subjects Transferred to t.o. Reading by their Teachers — 63

E15. Analysis of Errors Made in the t.o. Edition of Neale Test by 152 Experimental Group Subjects Transferred to t.o. Reading by their Teachers — 64

E16. Transfer of Learning from i.t.a. to t.o.—Accuracy — 66

E17. Transfer of Learning from i.t.a. to t.o.—Speed — 66

E18. Transfer of Learning from i.t.a. to t.o.—Comprehension — 66

E19. Reading in t.o. at mid-second year—Accuracy] — 67

E20. Reading in t.o. at mid-second year—Speed — 67

E21. Reading in t.o. at mid-second year—Comprehension — 67

E22. Word Recognition in t.o. at beginning of third year (middle of seventh term) — 68

E23. Reading in t.o. at end of three school years—Accuracy — 68

E24. Reading in t.o. at end of three school years—Speed — 68

E25. Reading in t.o. at end of three school years—Comprehension — 69

E26. Silent Reading Comprehension in t.o. at end of second and third school years — 69

E27. Staffordshire study of written composition Results of word analysis — 70

E28. t.o. spelling in Experimental (i.t.a.) and Control (t.o.) Groups as measured by Schonell Graded Word Spelling Test — 71

E29. Effectiveness of Manipulation of Hawthorne Effect in Control Group — 72

List of Graphs

page

Comparative Progress through Basic Reader Series over Ten Ranges of Achievement

Graph 1.	After One Year	73
Graph 2.	After 1⅓ Years	73
Graph 3.	After 2 Years	74
Graph 4.	After 2⅓ Years	74

Scores on Schonell Graded Word Reading Test over Ten Ranges of Achievement

Graph 5.	In 3rd Term	75
Graph 6.	In 5th Term	75

Scores on Neale Analysis of Reading Ability over Ten Ranges of Achievement

Graph 7.	Form C—After 1½ Years—Accuracy	76
Graph 8.	Form C—After 1½ Years—Reading Rate	76
Graph 9.	Form C—After 1½ Years—Comprehension	77
Graph 10.	Form A (in t.o. to both groups)—After 1½ Years—Accuracy	77
Graph 11.	Form A (in t.o. to both groups)—After 1½ Years—Reading Rate	78
Graph 12.	Form A (in t.o. to both groups)—After 1½ Years—Comprehension	78
Graph 13.	Experimental Group—Neale Form C (i.t.a.) and Form A (t.o.)—After 1½ Years—Accuracy	79
Graph 14.	Control Group—Neale Forms C and A (both in t.o.)—After 1½ Years—Accuracy	79
Graph 15.	Experimental Group—Neale Form C (i.t.a.) and Form A (t.o.)—After 1½ Years—Reading Rate	80
Graph 16.	Control Group—Neale Forms C and A (both in t.o.)—After 1½ Years—Reading Rate	80
Graph 17.	Experimental Group—Neale Form C (i.t.a.) and Form A (t.o.)—After 1½ Years—Comprehension	81

List of Graphs

		page
Graph 18.	Control Group—Neale Forms C and A (both in t.o.)—After $1\frac{1}{2}$ Years—Comprehension	81
Graph 19.	Form B—After 3 Years—Accuracy	82
Graph 20.	Experimental Group—Neale A—After $1\frac{1}{2}$ Years, Neale B—After 3 Years—Accuracy	82
Graph 21.	Control Group—Neale A—After $1\frac{1}{2}$ Years, Neale B—After 3 Years—Accuracy	83
Graph 22.	Form B—After 3 Years—Reading Rate	83
Graph 23.	Experimental Group—Neale A—After $1\frac{1}{2}$ Years, Neale B—After 3 Years—Reading Rate	84
Graph 24.	Control Group—Neale A—After $1\frac{1}{2}$ Years, Neale B—After 3 Years—Reading Rate	84
Graph 25.	Form B—After 3 Years—Comprehension	85
Graph 26.	Experimental Group—Neale A—After $1\frac{1}{2}$ Years, Neale B—After 3 Years—Comprehension	85
Graph 27.	Control Group—Neale A—After $1\frac{1}{2}$ Years, Neale B—After 3 Years—Comprehension	86

Schonell Graded Word Reading Test

Graph 28.	At Beginning of 3rd Year	86
Graph 29.	Experimental Group—Test in 5th Term (i.t.a.) and 7th Term (t.o.)	87
Graph 30.	Control Group—Test in 5th Term and 7th Term in t.o.	87

Silent Reading Comprehension Scores in t.o. for Both Groups on Standish N.S.45 Test, over Ten Ranges of Achievement

Graph 31.	After 2 Years	88
Graph 32.	After 3 Years	88

Schonell Graded Word Spelling Test Scores in t.o. for Both Groups over Ten Ranges of Achievement

Graph 33.	After $2\frac{1}{2}$ Years	89
Graph 34.	After $3\frac{1}{2}$ Years	89
Graph 35.	Experimental Group—After $2\frac{1}{2}$ Years and $3\frac{1}{2}$ Years	90
Graph 36.	Control Group—After $2\frac{1}{2}$ Years and $3\frac{1}{2}$ Years	90

Introduction

By H. L. ELVIN

Institute of Education, University of London.

THE Report that follows gives the first substantive account of experimental research work that both in its inception and during its progress has excited a good deal of public interest. Without a degree of such interest the work could not have been started and sustained; but the amount of this interest, and sometimes the nature of the popular discussion that has surrounded it, have inevitably obscured, for the time, the careful and objective examination of the problem of learning to read with an augmented alphabet that the research was designed to provide. In the nature of the case, interim statements, however interesting, could have no serious finality. Indeed, it is still too early to speak of finality. But it is hoped that this Report will enable colleagues in the world of educational research, as well as those concerned more generally with our educational procedures, to come to conclusions that are reasonably objective about the experiment itself and its findings and implications.

Perhaps I may be allowed in this Introduction to say something of the way in which the work came to be undertaken, since there have been numerous misunderstandings about this.

It was in the latter part of 1958 that Mr. (now Sir) James Pitman asked Dr. Wall, as Director of the National Foundation for Educational Research, and myself as Director of the Institute of Education in the University of London, whether we would be interested in an experiment to see whether children might learn to read more easily and effectively through an augmentation of our present alphabet instead of through our present very irregular orthography. He had already ventilated the matter in Parliament and elsewhere and had obtained a measure of influential support for at least seeing whether there was anything in this idea or not. Sir James prepared an article for the *Times Educational Supplement*, which appeared on 29 May 1959, and invited any one interested to get in touch with him.

This article was shown to us in draft and I consulted two of my colleagues who were close to this field of interest to say whether they

Research Report on the British Experiment with i.t.a.

thought we should go forward with the idea of an experiment. One advised against it on the grounds that to make children learn yet another set of symbols (which they would in any case have to unlearn later) would complicate their early education unreasonably, since they would be seeing the normal forms of writing all around them while learning these. And there was an additional danger that this device would encourage teachers and parents to press children to learn to read too early. My second colleague, apart from certain technical doubts he had about the proposal, felt that it would be very difficult to secure a properly controlled experiment, not least because teachers would be likely to be strong partisans for or against the new medium. Nevertheless, he said on balance that he would like to see the experiment tried, since in a matter of this sort experimental evidence would be of great interest. After much reflection on this far from unanimous counsel my more immediate colleagues and I decided that we would put up a proposal to the Committee of Management for a research experiment, backed by a grant from the firm of Pitman and Sons and a personal financial guarantee from Sir James himself. A Steering Committee was appointed, on which Sir Cyril Burt and Professor Fry of University College agreed to serve as well as Sir James Pitman and representatives of the Institute and the Foundation, and this Committee saw the work through its earlier stages.[1] Mr. John Downing was appointed Director of the Unit that would carry out the experiment and he took up his duties on 1 October 1960. In the first task of interesting teachers and education authorities in the idea of the experiment—irrespective of what its findings might be—we had the valuable public support of the then Minister of Education (Sir David Eccles), of Sir William Alexander (of the Association of Education Committees) and of Sir Ronald Gould (of the National Union of Teachers). I recall these historical details because they involve matters which should be kept clear.

First, the Institute (and I am sure the Foundation also) was interested in an idea, not a device. The idea was to test whether children could learn to read more effectively through an augmented alphabet, and it is perfectly reasonable to say (as Mr. Downing does) that this means that we were proposing to test, through a contrasting medium, whether the irregularity of application of the

[1] Acknowledgement should here be made of the valuable work carried out by the Committee, of which the following were members: Sir Cyril Burt, H. L. Elvin, D. B. Fry, J. M. Morris, W. R. Niblett, I. J. (*later* Sir James) Pitman, P. E. Vernon and W. D. Wall.

Introduction

English alphabet was a serious handicap in learning to read. Both the Institute and the Foundation had already shown some interest in this subject, since Dr. W. R. Lee (when a member of the staff of the Institute) had investigated the possible relationship between the irregularity of English spelling and difficulty in reading. He had come to the conclusion that it was doubtful if this was a serious cause of difficulty in reading, and his report was published by the N.F.E.R. in 1960. Nevertheless there was clearly room for a more widespread experiment in the schools concerned not simply with difficulty in reading but with initial learning to read.

This, then, was the important question we wished to investigate through a large-scale experiment. On the other hand there was never any doubt in the minds of those concerned with the launching of the work that the device we should use for testing this by contrast was the Augmented Roman alphabet, later styled i.t.a., devised by Sir James Pitman. This was there, ready to our hand. And it was the kind of device we needed. It is very important to understand that we needed an alternative alphabet that met two criteria. The medium we needed must on the one hand be so much more regular than traditional orthography that we could test whether the present irregularity of English was a serious handicap in learning; and on the other hand the medium must be close enough in appearance and nature to the present alphabet to make transfer possible at a later stage. We were not concerned with 'simplified spelling', but with a transitional learning through a modified medium. We made no claims that i.t.a. was the 'best' modification of the English alphabet. Indeed 'best' is a pointless epithet in this context. One has to ask, 'best for what?' This was difficult to make clear to some enthusiasts of linguistic reform. One linguist threatened me over the 'phone with dire consequences to the reputation of the Institute if we went on with our proposal to use i.t.a., and I obviously failed to convince him that we weren't advancing any claims for i.t.a. as 'the best' modification of English but wanted one appropriate to our experimental purpose, suiting both criteria; and were assured that we had that. We of course hoped that the experiment itself might suggest improvements that might be made in i.t.a. if it came to be widely adopted—and one or two modifications were indeed made—but some of us were equally conscious that if reformers in such a field were always chopping and changing there might only be confusion, and considerable frustration among those who were not persuaded that the main idea made much sense anyway. All that, however, was for the future for those concerned.

Research Report on the British Experiment with i.t.a.

The second point I must make (though one would hope there was hardly need for it) was that the Institute and the Foundation were not pre-disposed towards any particular outcome of the experiment. This point was put very clearly to Sir James Pitman, who concurred entirely. And I think I should record in the somewhat special circumstances that have attended this experiment—though it is almost insulting to a research worker—that Mr. Downing made it very clear to the committee that interviewed him for the appointment that he was entirely uncommitted in his own mind as to what the outcome might be.

The third point I would make is that we did understand from the first that this experiment would take place in real living communities with their schools, not in a laboratory, and that this involved very difficult problems of control not all of which we might be able to surmount to our reasonable satisfaction. In particular there was worry about the Hawthorne Effect. Unless we interested teachers and education officers in the project we should not be able to do the experimental research. Unless we could persuade parents that it was reasonable for them to agree, too, it would be wrong for us to press the matter. All this involved an initial effort of persuasion that not surprisingly seemed to some observers to have something of a 'missionary' tone. It did work up interest in the experiment, but this had to be done. As Mr. Downing explains, steps were taken to bring into play something of an equivalent Hawthorne Effect in the control groups. No one can be confident that this element is ever ruled out in a field experiment of this kind. What we can ask is whether when allowance has been made for a possible effect of this sort the differences between two ways of learning or working are still significant.

There is no doubt that the suspicion of 'promotion' hung over the research during its progress. There were of course those not in the research team, who 'believed' in i.t.a. and had every right to say so. But so far as the research workers themselves were concerned there was still a dilemma. If Mr. Downing or any of his colleagues spoke with some enthusiasm of what they were doing, even if they cautioned that first findings were provisional, that was 'promotion'. It is not easy to throw your whole energy into a piece of work and not show some zeal about it. However, it was to deal with this difficulty that Sir James Pitman started the i.t.a. Foundation, which could 'promote' as its members wished, while the Reading Research Unit stuck to research.

Introduction

Just as there were enthusiasts for the work in the schools, so there were those who were quite sure that the experiment was wrongheaded and possibly dangerous. One very common misconception was that i.t.a. would make children begin to read too soon. It of course left the question as to when a child should begin to read quite unanswered. All it did was to investigate whether, when a child did begin, it could make progress more easily and more effectively than with traditional orthography. It was odd to find some of the educational 'progressives' failing to make this distinction, though assuredly they could not really have meant that when children did begin to read the process should be made more difficult than it need be.

So, from one side or another, the experiment has been under a running fire. I would only venture the comment that if educational research confines itself to what is safe and can be performed in conditions that are easy to control, it will fail in its duty to the country at the present time. The reason is the simple one that many of the questions the public is rightly concerned about can only be dealt with in field conditions, where the variables are numerous and tricky. Years ago we should have begun to study the comparative educational effects of a comprehensive and a selective secondary school plan, as the Swedes have. But this was a 'hot' subject, from both sides. Yet it is the one all-important question in secondary school structure about which the public is concerned. In such investigations, undertaken because they are important, and undertaken in full knowledge of the difficulties of really controlled work, the greatest effort must be made to keep a proper research objectivity. The i.t.a. experimental research has been something of a pilot venture in this respect. Some of the shortcomings are very evident to the research workers themselves. Others will be pointed out. As to the effort to maintain objectivity and careful standards the Report speaks for itself.

Perhaps now I may be permitted some further remarks that will, I think, be of interest to any one who is cherishing a research project in education and wonders how it is that some of them 'get off the ground' while others do not. This, too, may be of interest to heads of institutions who get a few headaches because some projects that get off the ground don't find it easy to stay up (I will refrain from saying anything about the cross-fires in which such persons may find themselves involved, conscious that they are laymen in such particular disputes much more than professionals).

Research Report on the British Experiment with i.t.a.

In education, which concerns us all, not all new ideas deserving investigation come from professional 'educators'. Any idea that does not is unlikely to get far unless some one believes in it, and moreover has considerable skill and a position of some influence to bring people round to the feeling that it might be worth trying. In all proposals that bear on the average man an immense inertia has to be overcome. We now accept the simple idea of summer time, but it took William Willett all his life to get a government even to look at it, and he only succeeded in this country because of the exigencies of the World War I. Sir James Pitman, following in the footsteps of his famous grandfather Sir Isaac Pitman, has been the 'missionary' of i.t.a. as a device for initial reading, and quite obviously without both his persistence and his skill in preparing people's minds for an investigation nothing would have happened. The experiment took place because he had mobilized enough support in educational quarters for trying the proposal in practice, and those who think the experiment has been worthwhile owe a great deal to the people who in the early days said they thought it would be, whatever the findings.

This kind of experiment, however, needed more. For one thing it needed the help of publishers. Sir James is the head of a publishing firm, but he made it clear from the start that, so far as he was concerned, any publisher could benefit equally from any possibilities he saw in such work. The experiment owed a great deal to the fact that early on, Mr. Mackenzie-Wood, the Chairman of James Nisbet and Co., agreed that there should be an i.t.a. version of the popular *Janet and John* series of readers so that comparisons might be made with learning by the t.o. text. And later, when the need for many publications in the Book Corners of classes using i.t.a. became clear, many other publishers helped.

There was, therefore, a necessary but rather unusual combination of circumstances that enabled this experiment to be started. But of course one other thing is always necessary: money. The Institute has no funds of its own for educational research. The i.t.a. research could begin only because support was assured from the firm of Pitman and Sons and Sir James himself, as already mentioned; from a number of benefactors, of whom the late W. Howard Samuel, Associated Television and Boots Pure Drug Co. Ltd. were among the most generous; and from a number of individuals, of whom the Directors of Education were the most encouraging. Very soon, however, it became clear that we had most seriously underestimated, especially in the matter of the provision of reading materials. For the main

Introduction

experiment the Ford Foundation came most generously to our rescue, not least because this work was proving of interest in the United States and they wished the fullest information and assistance to be made available over there. We also had financial support, at a particularly difficult time, from the Ministry of Education (as it was then styled); from the Grant Foundation (via the Educational Records Bureau) of New York; and from The Fund for the Advancement of Education. And as other lines of investigation opened up which it would have been foolish to ignore while we were in a position to collect data and use data we had collected, others, and especially the Nuffield Foundation, came to our assistance. It still remains painfully true that had more money been available the research design could have been improved and the work done more satisfactorily. There are no doubt those who will say that these tales are commonplace in university research, as indeed they are, and that this is a test of the seriousness of effort of any university research workers who think something worth doing. Personally, I wonder if this is the way in which a great nation should have its research financed.

One doubt about the acceptance of the project by the Institute was that if we had had generally available research funds we might not have chosen the i.t.a. research for high priority. This, in the circumstances of that time, was almost certainly true, rightly or wrongly. It is galling, if you want to work out anything like a research policy for an institution, to find that you have two lists of priorities: one, the list that fits what you think your institution should do and can best do, and a second and quite different list which puts projects in order of their success in attracting financial support from outside. I feel this as strongly as any one. But I do not go so far as to say that one should not go ahead with, for instance, project five on the first list because projects one to four have not attracted grants. All one can do is to make as sure as one can that a project is worthwhile in itself, and that a reasonable balance over the whole field is kept.

Personally, I am sure that this i.t.a. experiment whatever the findings are or might have been, was worth doing. In spite of the almost daily difficulties they have had to surmount, the persistence of Sir James Pitman and the almost heroic energy and fertile research skill of Mr. Downing and his fellow workers have been justified and have led to an experiment that is full of interest. Nothing I have said is to be taken as an attempt to disarm criticism. The Report

Research Report on the British Experiment with i.t.a.

is now before those who are interested and, except that behind it is still more unpublished material for which there is no space, it stands on its own feet. I would only hope that it shows, in conjunction with the constructive criticisms that will no doubt be made and welcomed, that an extensive field investigation of a really significant question can be both of theoretical interest and of practical use in education.

Research Report
on the
British Experiment with i.t.a.

JOHN DOWNING

CHAPTER I

Historical Background and Origins of the i.t.a. Research

THE major concern of this report is the research which has been conducted in Britain between 1961 and 1966 into the effects of simplifying and regularizing English orthography upon the learning of reading and writing. A forthcoming publication by the present author[1] will contain a comprehensive account of the historical background, design and development of Sir James Pitman's Initial Teaching Alphabet (i.t.a.) as an instance of such simplification and regularization, as well as a review of previous investigations into other reformed (simplified and regularized) writing-systems.[2] The bibliography at the end of this report includes selected references for readers interested in studying these aspects of the development of English orthography.

The view that the traditional orthography (t.o.) of English is an important cause of difficulty in the teaching and learning of reading in English-speaking countries has frequently been advanced during the past four centuries. Advocates of reformed orthographies for English have usually stressed one or more of these three needed improvements:

(1) augmentation of the alphabet;
(2) regularization of the spelling;
(3) reduction in the number of alternatives or of redundant symbols in the writing-system.

Those, past and present, who have devoted their minds to a reformed orthography, have usually assumed that the acceptance of their proposals for change must imply a complete and permanent change-over (reading, writing and printing) by the entire population, and their attempts to provide the means to achieve spelling reform have been based on this assumption. In contrast, the i.t.a. writing-system developed by Sir James Pitman was deliberately designed as

[1] DOWNING, J. A. (1967). *Evaluating the Initial Teaching Alphabet*. London: Cassell.
[2] The term 'writing-system' refers to a system of writing used to represent in 'ink' the system of 'air' which is the primary language form.

Research Report on the British Experiment with i.t.a.

a *transitional* writing-system—a grading-device for use only by beginners in the initial stages of learning to read, after which it may be discarded as they make a transition to reading in t.o. It is this special transitional characteristic which differentiates i.t.a. from most other reformed writing-systems for English.

An opportunity to conduct a scientific investigation of the effects of English orthography on the early stages of the development of literacy skills was presented by the decision in 1960 of the University of London Institute of Education and the National Foundation for Educational Research in England and Wales, to give their joint support to an experiment with a simplified and regularized alphabet. Sir Ronald Gould, Secretary of the National Union of Teachers, and Sir William Alexander, Secretary of the Association of Education Committees also gave their blessing to this research. Earlier, in 1953, the Minister of Education had promised her 'interest and goodwill'[1] for such an experiment in response to Dr. Mont Follick's question in the House of Commons asking if she would state her policy towards proposals by a competent research organization to investigate possible improvements in the teaching of reading by means of 'a system of simplified spelling'.[1] There were other simplified writing-systems which could have been tested but it was decided by the committee set up to guide the project that Pitman's Augmented Roman alphabet (A.R.—later i.t.a.) should be the example of such writing-systems which should be used to investigate the fundamental question—Is the complexity and irregularity of the traditional orthography of English an important cause of difficulty in learning to read? Accordingly, the Reading Research Unit was established in 1960 to investigate (in the words of the Institute of Education's appeal pamphlet) 'the early stages of learning to read, when the matter to be read is printed in a special form alleged to be easy to learn and leading easily to a full reading skill'.

---

[1] *Parliamentary Debates* (Hansard). 7 May 1953. London: H.M.S.O.

CHAPTER II

The First i.t.a. Experiment—Aims, Methodology and Design

1. Aims of the First i.t.a. Experiment

IN September 1960, a design for an investigation of the effectiveness of the Initial Teaching Alphabet for beginning reading was prepared. Because the scope of the evaluation programme of i.t.a. had, necessarily, to be limited by the funds available, it was decided to confine the investigation to the study of a few basic, practical questions which appeared to be of greatest importance to the teachers and administrators who were considering using i.t.a. in Infant Schools. A full statement of these questions and the related hypotheses will be published elsewhere[1] but for the present purposes they may be summarized as follows:

Question I: Can children learn to read more easily with i.t.a. than they can with traditional orthography (t.o.)?
Two major hypotheses are related to this question:
Hypothesis 1: Because of the reduction in the volume of learning in i.t.a. as compared with t.o., children in i.t.a. classes should make significantly more rapid progress through their basic reader series.
Hypothesis 2: Because of the greater regularity of graphemephoneme relations in i.t.a. as compared with t.o., pupils learning to read with i.t.a. should achieve significantly higher scores on reading tests in which lower-order decoding skills have an especially important role to play.

Question II: Can pupils transfer their training in reading i.t.a. to reading in t.o.?
The hypothesis is:
Hypothesis 3: Because of i.t.a.'s design as a transitional alphabet, in i.t.a. classes, reading achievements in t.o. should not be inferior to previous achievements in i.t.a. once fluency in i.t.a. has been established.

[1] DOWNING, J. A. (1967). *Evaluating the Initial Teaching Alphabet.* London: Cassell.

Research Report on the British Experiment with i.t.a.

Question III: After the whole process of beginning with i.t.a. and transferring to t.o., are reading attainments in t.o. superior to what they would have been without the intervention of i.t.a.?
The major hypothesis here is that:

Hypothesis 4: Through positive transfer from i.t.a. *learning to* t.o. *learning, pupils who have first learned to read with* i.t.a. *and then made the transition to* t.o. *should read the latter with significantly greater accuracy, speed and comprehension than pupils who have not used* i.t.a. *in the beginning.*

Question IV: Will children's written compositions be more fluent with the simpler i.t.a. code for speech? (i.e. will the gap between their spoken and written vocabularies be narrowed?)
Two hypotheses were to be tested here:

Hypothesis 5: Because i.t.a. *also simplifies and regularizes the encoding operation, the written compositions of* i.t.a. *pupils should be longer than those of children who begin reading in* t.o.

Hypothesis 6: The written vocabulary of i.t.a. *pupils should be more extensive than that of their* t.o. *counterparts.*

Question V: How will children's later attainments in t.o. spelling be influenced by their earlier experiences of reading and writing the different spellings of i.t.a.?
The early experiences with the regular grapheme-phoneme relations of i.t.a. should also produce positive transfer to t.o. spelling. Therefore, the hypothesis is that:

Hypothesis 7: Spelling attainments in t.o. *after the transition stage should be superior in classes where* i.t.a. *was used for the beginning stage.*

Findings relevant to these hypotheses are given and discussed in Chapter III.

2. Methodology of the First i.t.a. Experiment

'Large-scale experiments conducted in the normal social setting involve many complex problems of design, analysis and interpretation. These arise from the complexity of the educational situation in which there are many factors which are either known to affect attainment or which are believed to do so.'[1]

[1] DOWNING, J. A. and JONES, B. (1966). 'Some problems of evaluating i.t.a.—a second experiment'. *Educational Research*, VIII, 100-114.

The First i.t.a. Experiment—Aims, Methodology and Design

Although the aim in this research was to conduct a rigorous experimental investigation of the above questions, a general principle that the evaluation programme *should be immediately meaningful to teachers and administrators* influenced the research design and choice of instruments.

For example, for the first i.t.a. experiment this principle led to the adoption of the type of design which French has termed the 'Field Experiment'.[1] It was conducted under representative everyday-life classroom conditions rather than under specially contrived laboratory conditions. A difficult problem in such large-scale field experiments as this in educational research is the control of 'incidental variables', i.e. those factors in the situation, excluding the one to be studied, which may affect attainment. One method of classifying such 'incidental variables' is in terms of *source* of variation, as below:

(1) *Pupil Variables*
   (*a*) *Individual*
      e.g. age, sex, intelligence
   (*b*) *Home background*
      e.g. socio-economic class

(2) *School Variables*
   (*a*) *Tangible*
      e.g. size of school, pupil-teacher ratio
   (*b*) *Intangible*
      e.g. direction of policy by headteacher, 'tone' of school

(3) *Teacher Variables*
      e.g. experience, personality

(4) *Teacher-School Interaction Variables*
      e.g. curriculum, method

Cutting across the above type of classification, there is another division of the variables into two categories; variables which are a normal part of the educational situation, and those which may arise as a consequence of the experiment.

In the first of these two categories one could include pupil background variables such as age, sex and intelligence; school variables such as size of school and pupil-teacher ratio; and teacher variables such as, for example, experience and personality.

---

[1] FRENCH, J. R. P. (Jnr.) (1954). 'Experiments in field settings'. In: FESTINGER, L. and KATZ, D., eds. *Research Methods in the Behavioral Sciences.* London: Staples Press.

Research Report on the British Experiment with i.t.a.

A further distinction might be made within this first category, between variables which are related to the writing-system (i.t.a. or t.o.) and others which are not. The attitudes of parents, teachers, and pupils to the writing-system might be considered a variable of this kind.

In the second category are included those variables which arise from the experiment itself, from circumstances incidental to its setting-up or its administration. For example, it has been claimed that when members of a group become the subjects of an experiment there is an improvement in motivation, and consequently in performance, by such members—this is the celebrated 'Hawthorne Effect' which takes its name from the Hawthorne Works in Chicago where, between 1927 and 1933, this effect was reported to have been observed in the course of experiments involving employees of the Western Electric Company. How far one can generalize from this industrial study to the dynamics of teacher and pupil groups within the British educational system is uncertain. This problem and its relevance to the present research is discussed at some length in a recent article.[1]

One cannot claim that complete control was established over all the variables discussed above, but by initial matching, as described in the present chapter, and later statistical analysis, a determined effort was made to limit bias arising from such variables.

In this present analysis of the data equal numbers of children from matched control and experimental schools were selected by a random procedure. This approach reduced the number of subjects involved in the analysis but led to a better match between experimental and control populations, although, as will be pointed out in Chapter III, some bias involving incidental variables still showed itself. As will be seen, this bias can be considered to favour the Control Groups in certain of the tests.

In the first experiments, for reasons to be explained later in this chapter, all the teachers taking part volunteered specifically for the experimental or the control side of the investigation and it was not possible with available resources to attempt the difficult, if not impossible in the present state of our knowledge, task of evaluating

[1] DOWNING, J. A. and JONES, B. (1966). 'Some problems of evaluating i.t.a.—a second experiment'. *Educational Research*, VIII, 100-114.

The First i.t.a. Experiment—Aims, Methodology and Design

teacher-training, experience, personality and ability in control and experimental classes. In a second experiment, however, begun in 1963, and already reported elsewhere,[1] an attempt was made to control the teacher variable by arranging for the experimental and control classes to be shared by two teachers. In this second study an attempt was also made to obtain more rigorous control of the Hawthorne Effect by another method. By agreement with Local Education Authorities and schools, visits by outside persons to control and experimental classes were restricted and equated and the classes did not receive any publicity.

The results from this second study are, so far, in agreement with those reported in the present volume.

3. Design of the First i.t.a. Experiment

The basic design of the initial experiment was as follows:

(a) *An Experimental Group* of classes began reading with the basic readers and other supplementary books printed in i.t.a.

(b) *A Control Group* of classes began reading with the same basic readers printed in t.o. A few of these control classes were in the same school building as an experimental class, but most were in different schools. In this Control Group an attempt was made to create an artificial 'Hawthorne Effect' to match that which seemed likely to occur in the Experimental Group (for technique employed see Section 8—*Procedure*, below).

(c) A second *Special Control Group* consisted of children one year older who had entered the control group schools one year before the experiment started. This second Special Control Group differed from the first Control Group in that no attempt was made to induce an artificial Hawthorne Effect. A comparison between the Control Group proper and this second Control Group provided a check on the effectiveness of the attempt to induce Hawthorne Effect artificially (hereafter, 'Control Group' refers to the Control Group proper in which the attempt was made to induce an artificial Hawthorne Effect). The hypotheses related to the questions set out in the first section of this chapter were tested by comparing the attainments of the Experimental and Control Groups. The design of

[1] DONWING, J. A. and JONES, B. (1966). 'Some problems of evaluating i.t.a.—a second experiment'. *Educational Research*, VIII, 100-114.

Research Report on the British Experiment with i.t.a.

this research included an attempt to match the Experimental Group and the Control Group on intelligence, age, sex, social class, size of school, pupil-teacher ratio, urban/rural location, type of school organization (Infants only, Infants and Juniors combined) and certain school amenities. Details of the matching procedures are given on page 11 and the extent to which they proved effective is shown in Chapter III.

4. Populations in the Initial Experiment

In Britain each headteacher is free to decide on the methods to be used in his or her school. The Director of Education may ask his headteachers to *consider* using a method, but he does not command teachers to use it. In these circumstances the Experimenter had much less difficulty in persuading Directors to co-operate than in persuading headteachers to try i.t.a. It was decided that i.t.a. was such an innovation in a conservative climate, that a random sampling procedure was impracticable because most schools chosen would have refused to co-operate. As the project, therefore, depended on voluntary participation, it was necessary to seek volunteers in selected areas—some to try i.t.a. in an Experimental Group, and others to demonstrate in a Control Group that t.o. was quite adequate without any modifications such as i.t.a. With this sampling problem it was clearly of importance to match the Experimental and Control Groups carefully on variables of known importance and/or to analyse, subsequently, the variance between experimental and control populations on such variables.

Recruitment to the Experimental and Control Groups was made by approaching Directors of Education. The selected areas were chosen in consultation with the then Ministry of Education, the aim being to provide a cross-section of the school population in areas reasonably accessible to the Experimenter and his assistants. When the areas had been chosen, the Directors of Education concerned were approached personally by the Experimenter (The Head of the Reading Research Unit) to request a meeting with headteachers in the Local Education Authority (L.E.A.). In 1961, seven L.E.A. Directors agreed to help, and six of these seven L.E.A.s provided subjects in 1961.

The original aim was to recruit children to each of the Experimental and Control Groups in sufficiently large numbers to facilitate later matching. However, i.t.a. seemed to be regarded as such a

The First i.t.a. Experiment—Aims, Methodology and Design

bizarre idea before it had been tried that it proved a difficult task to find headteachers willing to try it. Therefore in September 1961 when the experiment was launched, only twenty schools were found to be willing and able to introduce i.t.a. for beginning reading. It was less difficult to find volunteer headteachers for the Control Group who believed, not unreasonably, that the experiment would show that t.o. was quite adequate for the teaching of reading in their schools. Thirty-three such control schools joined the research in September 1961.

It was decided to recruit schools to the research until sufficient classes had been obtained to provide a range in which reasonable matching on background variables would be possible between Experimental and Control Groups. In the meantime, volunteers to both groups were accepted and encouraged to use the appropriate i.t.a. or t.o. medium and materials (see Section 8—*Procedure* below).

In 1962, recruitment of schools to the research continued. It proved easier to obtain volunteers to use i.t.a. in the second year, but prejudice against i.t.a. still hampered recruitment of subjects, and it was not until the academic year 1963-64 that schools had volunteered for each group in sufficient numbers for the two groups to be matched satisfactorily.

Tables 1 and 2 show the number of schools and pupils in the various L.E.A.s which have contributed subjects to this analysis of the data of the first i.t.a. experiment.

TABLE 1

NUMBER OF SCHOOLS AND CLASSES IN FIRST i.t.a. EXPERIMENT

	Totals: Overall number of Classes Recruited		Schools which could not be matched		MATCHED SAMPLE			
					Matched External (Schools)		Matched Internal (Classes)	
Year	Exp.	Con.	Exp.	Con.	Exp.	Con.	Exp.	Con.
1961 ..	20	33	9	19	11	13	—	1
1962 ..	56	23	39	9	10	8	7	6
1963 ..	13	13	—	—	12	12	1	1
TOTAL	89	69	48	28	33	33	8	8

TABLE 2

Maximum number of Experimental and Control Subjects in Matched Groups possible from the Matched Schools or Classes in the present Analysis of Data from the First i.t.a. Experiment

L.E.A. No.	L.E.A.	EXPERIMENTAL Schools/Classes	Pupils	CONTROL Schools/Classes	Pupils
1	Bedfordshire	1	29	3	40
2	Belfast	1	37	1	37
3	Blackburn	3	40	–	–
4	Bolton	4	80	3	46
5	Burton-on-Trent	1	10	–	–
6	Cheshire	1	9	–	–
7	Dundee	–	–	1	31
8	Edinburgh	2	67	2	67
9	Exeter	1	17	–	–
10	Harrow	–	–	1	17
11	Hull	–	–	1	23
12	Huntingdonshire	1	5	–	–
13	Leicestershire	3	49	6	130
14	Irlam & Urmston	–	–	1	10
15	Newcastle-under-Lyme[1]	1	18	–	–
16	Oldham	7	193	5	125
17	Rochdale	1	36	3	100
18	Southend	1	17	1	17
19	Staffordshire	4	87	7	127
20	Stoke-on-Trent	4	87	6	103
21	Walsall	2	27	–	–
22	West Riding, Yorkshire[2]	1	12	–	–
23	Wigan	1	23	–	–
24	Wolverhampton	1	30	–	–
	TOTALS	41	873	41	873

[1] An Excepted District of Staffordshire.
[2] An Excepted Borough (Keighley).

The First i.t.a. Experiment—Aims, Methodology and Design

5. Matching of Experimental with Control Groups
ENVIRONMENTAL VARIABLES

In this first experiment on i.t.a. the initial matching of the two groups was attempted on seven background variables which have been found to be significant environmental factors in previous research on reading in Britain:

(a) *Urban/Rural Location*;

(b) *Type of School Organization* (Infants only school, i.e. no children over age seven, or Junior and Infants combined—i.e., children in same school till age eleven);

(c) *Size of School* (number of infants on roll);

(d) *Pupil/Teacher Ratio* (number of infants on roll/number of full-time teachers—two half-time teachers counted as one full-time);

(e) *Amenities of the School Building.* This assessment was based on that used by Morris[1] and points were given as follows:

		No. of points
1.	Date of building (after 1920)	1
2.	Staffroom	1
3.	(Hall used as classroom)	1
	(Hall not used as classroom or canteen)	3
4.	Large rooms with good windows	1
5.	Modern furniture	1
6.	Sinks in classrooms	1
7.	(Separate stockrooms and plenty of cupboards)	2
	(No stockroom but plenty of cupboards)	1
8.	Electric light	1
9.	(Good sanitation)	1
	(Hot water)	1
10.	Separate pegs in cloakroom	1
11.	Infant playground	1
12.	Good location	1
13.	Pleasant general appearance	1

(f) *Minimum Age* when children may be admitted to the school;

---

[1] Morris' original schedule was derived from 'a list of the features of school buildings which, from practical experience, were considered to have the most marked effect in school life'. See: MORRIS, J. M. (1959). *Reading in the Primary School*, p. 31 and pp. 139-140. N.F.E.R. Research Reports. London: Newnes.

Research Report on the British Experiment with i.t.a.

(g) *Social Class* (Fathers' occupations—Registrar General's[1] categories) of children entering the school a year previous to the beginning of the research, or, for the September 1963 classes, on teachers' estimates of the school population.

Thus pupils could be coded on the above variables into seven environmental categories. Of these seven variables which were taken into account in matching prior to the beginning of the experiment proper, two, 'Minimum Age' and 'Social Class' became 'pupil variables' (see below) as soon as information concerning the children actually involved in the experiment became available. The 'Minimum Age' variable was replaced by the actual age of the children concerned and the estimated likely social class distributions by the actual distributions pertaining to the research populations. For each critical test of attainment, subjects were discarded by random procedure to equalize the contributions of each school (or class) in the matched experimental and control pairs, and the data in respect of the five pupil variables was analysed to determine the comparability of the samples. These pupil variables on which comparability of the two groups was sought are as follows:

PUPIL VARIABLES

(a) (i) *'Intelligence'*—*(non-verbal)* and (ii) *'Vocabulary'*

All children in both groups were tested on entering school. Raven's Coloured Progressive Matrices[2] and Raven's Crichton Vocabulary Scale[3] were administered individually. (See Section 8—*Procedure* below.)

(b) *Social Class*

The Registrar General's list was used to classify fathers' occupations as supplied by teachers or from medical record cards. Where the information was ambiguous it was either not used or, in some cases, an arbitrary rule was adopted, e.g. 'engineer' was allocated to Class 3 unless additional information indicated that a higher class was appropriate.

(c) *Age*

In respect of each critical test of attainment, the distribution of ages in each group at the time of testing was compared.

[1] Census of England and Wales 1951, General Report—1958.
[2] RAVEN, J. C. (1949), *Coloured Progressive Matrices*. London: H. K. Lewis.
[3] RAVEN, J. C. (1950). *Crichton Vocabulary Scale*. London: H. K. Lewis.

The First i.t.a. Experiment—Aims, Methodology and Design

(*d*) *Sex*

The two groups were similarly compared in respect of the ratio of boys and girls in them.

6. Materials

As has been mentioned above, the 'Field Experiment' approach requires the maintenance of everyday-life conditions as far as is possible within the limits imposed by the need for control of variables and it was decided, accordingly, that the series of basic readers most popular in Britain should be used. The experimental classes had their *Janet and John*[1] books printed in i.t.a. while the control classes continued to use *Janet and John* books in t.o. In addition to the basic readers, the teaching apparatus published with this series was also produced in i.t.a. for the experimental classes.

In British Infant Schools, much emphasis is placed on the importance of the 'Book Corner' (classroom library), and it was recognized from the outset that, if the experimental conditions were to be representative of the normal approach in this respect, it would be necessary to produce many books in i.t.a. for the Book Corner.

Making i.t.a. free for use by all cleared the way for publishers to produce i.t.a. editions of their books. This freedom to use i.t.a., without proviso, was made plain in the pamphlet issued by the University of London Institute of Education and the National Foundation for Educational Research in England and Wales in 1960 when they appealed for moral and/or financial support. Under the heading 'NO COPYRIGHT' it was stated that 'The particular alphabet used above may be obtained (in 12 pt.) from The Monotype Corporation, 43 Fetter Lane, E.C.4. Any designers' rights have been freed for all time for unrestricted use by all'. Nevertheless, to provide a reasonably representative i.t.a. Book Corner proved a costly and time-consuming task. For example, publishers had to be persuaded to consider an i.t.a. edition of one or more of the books on their lists. The texts had to be transliterated and the Experimenter became involved in much of the other detailed work of bringing out the books, e.g. proof-reading in quantity.

It must be recognized that the matching of the conditions in respect of materials fell short of the ideal in the first experiment. The i.t.a. classes had new and fresh readers but suffered from a restricted choice of Book Corner materials, many of which were of

---

[1] The Experimenter wishes to acknowledge the generous way in which Mr. Mackenzie-Wood, Chairman of the publishers of the *Janet and John* series, Messrs. James Nisbet & Co., co-operated in this research.

the improvised 'paste-in' variety. The t.o. classes often had 'tired' copies of the readers but had a much wider selection of materials for the Book Corner. Possibly these differences may have balanced each other out to some extent, but this must remain a matter of conjecture.

In accordance with the aim to make a 'Field Experiment' approach, other aspects of the child's environment in respect of books were considered. In order not to disturb normal conditions in the Experimental Group it was decided not to attempt to isolate children learning i.t.a. from their normal t.o. environment. If the teacher normally used reference books in the Infants' classroom which could not be produced in i.t.a. by reason of cost, these were not removed but remained in the classroom in their normal t.o. edition. Also, of course, children in the i.t.a. classes continued to meet t.o. at home and in the streets. In respect of the early-learning stage, the i.t.a. children were thus at a disadvantage because they did not have their classroom experience reinforced to the same extent as the t.o. group by experiences with printed English outside school. To offset this in some degree, i.t.a. books were made available outside school for the Experimental Group by public libraries in the locality, and headteachers arranged for parents of the i.t.a. children to buy i.t.a. books for birthdays and for Christmas.

Essentially, then, the difference between the Experimental Group and the Control Group was not one of a pure contrast between the former using i.t.a. materials and the latter using t.o. materials, for the Experimental Group had experience of both i.t.a. and t.o. while the Control Group's experience was limited to t.o. Probably the Experimental Group's experience of both i.t.a. and t.o. may have had an effect on these children's ability to transfer from i.t.a. to t.o. at the later stage, but in judging the results of the earlier phase, when the Experimental Group was using the i.t.a. basic series and being tested on i.t.a. tests, it must be taken into account that the Experimental Group seems likely to have been at a disadvantage in terms of frequency of exposure to the i.t.a. letter- and word-forms they were learning.

In the first two years of the initial experiment these were the conditions with regard to the relative availability of i.t.a. and t.o. materials. By the third year (1963), when thirteen experimental i.t.a. schools entered the research to make the total of eighty-nine,[1] the

---

[1] This number refers only to the number of schools using i.t.a. in this first experiment. A recent survey shows nearly 1,800 schools in Britain using i.t.a.

The First i.t.a. Experiment—Aims, Methodology and Design

i.t.a. book situation had improved. Now, in 1966, a much greater variety of books[1] is available in i.t.a. and it would be possible to provide a more adequate i.t.a. book environment for an experimental group.

7. The Teachers and their Methods

In the initial experiment, methods of teaching were not prescribed for the i.t.a. Experimental Group or the Control Group. Teachers were asked only that they should not change their normal methods but should continue with their usual approach to the teaching of reading. Complete information on the teaching methods actually used is not available, but observations to date suggest that both groups are representative of normal practice in Britain. Like most of their professional colleagues, the teachers in both i.t.a. and t.o. classes used an eclectic approach to reading, i.e. 'mixed methods'. For instance, in their first year of the initial experiment, only one of the twenty i.t.a. schools used a formal phonic method from the start. As is usual in this country, the majority of teachers began with a Look-Say approach and introduced Phonics later as the children became ready to learn to use this tool.

Similarly, teachers in both i.t.a. and control groups were asked to preserve their normal practice in all other respects, e.g. reading-readiness, classroom organization, formal-informal approach, and proportion of time given to reading.

There could, of course, be no 'normal practice' as regards the transfer from i.t.a. to t.o. in the experimental classes, and some suggestions had to be given as to how children could be helped to make a smooth transition from i.t.a. to t.o. in reading and writing, and spelling. Further details on the methods used are given in Section 8—*Procedure* which follows.

Thus in this initial experiment there has been a matching on teaching methods only in the general sense that in both groups the traditional freedom of the teacher to use the methods she finds most appropriate for her class has been maintained. The weakness of this aspect of the initial experiment is that a number of variables known to be of importance in reading are not under deliberate and direct control. On the other hand, this matching of the liberal approach to teaching methods in both groups is a strength in terms

---

[1] For a list of more than 500 books published in i.t.a., see: *i.t.a. Books for the Teacher and the Child*. Available from the National Book League, 7 Albemarle Street, London, W.1.

of its fulfilment of the 'Field Experiment' aim to reproduce as far as possible the real-life school situation in this country, for it is probable that variations in emphasis in teaching methods may be balanced out in the quite large samples used.

It is also very important to consider the quality of the teaching. How able are the teachers? How well-trained are they? How much teaching experience have they had? Again, these could not be matched in *the first and major experiment*. In a second and subsidiary experiment[1] on i.t.a., variables such as teaching quality and methods have been controlled more rigorously in an attempt to provide data for judging the importance of variables in the first experiment.

8. Procedure

In 1960 preparatory work for the i.t.a. experiment was undertaken, e.g. review of previous research in this field, determination of the experimental design, and approaches to publishers to produce i.t.a. materials. In September 1961 the experiment began in the schools.

(a) Recruitment of Subjects

The first step in the actual field work was to meet Directors of Education in the selected Local Education Authorities. This was followed by a meeting of headteachers at which the Experimenter outlined his proposal for the i.t.a. experiment. Headteachers were asked to consult their class teachers and to decide whether to volunteer for the i.t.a. Experimental or t.o. Control Group or not to take part at all. The Head of the Reading Research Unit visited control and experimental schools if the headteachers felt that this would help class teachers to appreciate what they were being asked to undertake.

(b) Teacher-Training in the Use of i.t.a.

The teachers who were to use i.t.a. had to learn the new characters of i.t.a. and the spelling system which is an essential part of the new medium. To make this possible, the Experimenter arranged with the Local Education Authorities for teachers to attend a two-day course on i.t.a. These two days were not usually consecutive. Generally a one-day meeting would be held and then, after an interval of about a week, the second day of the course would be given.

[1] DOWNING, J. A. and JONES, B. (1966). 'Some problems of evaluating i.t.a.—a second experiment'. *Educational Research*, VIII, 100-114.

The First i.t.a. Experiment—Aims, Methodology and Design

This interval enabled teachers to practise writing and spelling in i.t.a. and to discuss any difficulties at the second meeting. The content of these two-day courses on i.t.a. should be considered in judging the results of this experiment. It contained the following aspects (not presented in this order, but suitably broken up to maintain interest, etc.):

(i) *The i.t.a. Characters and Spelling*
This was the most important part of the course. Clearly teachers cannot teach with i.t.a. if they have not mastered the system themselves, and considerable effort on the part of the teachers was required both during the course and in their 'homework'.
The teachers were taught i.t.a. through a sound-to-symbol approach. A phonemic analysis of English was made and the ways of writing each phoneme in i.t.a. were described. It was emphasized that i.t.a. was *not a phonetic alphabet* but a *teaching alphabet*. The design of i.t.a for transfer was outlined and the consequent need for the small number of alternatives and irregularities within i.t.a. (relatively small in comparison with the number in t.o.) were explained. The learning of these i.t.a. spelling conventions took most of the time needed for this important aspect of the course. It was pointed out that this need to learn the i.t.a. spelling rules applied *only* to the teachers and *not* to the children. For example, teachers need to know that z is used for the initial sound in zꝏ, zebra, zip because it is written *z* in t.o. but that ș ('zess') is used in cases where *z* is not used for this same sound in t.o. (e.g. *houses, feeds, cabs*) in order to maintain similarity of configuration for transfer purposes (i.e. houșeș, feedș, cabș). Children would not be required to differentiate z and ș, but teachers needed to do this if they were to reproduce words in the same spellings as those found in the publishers' i.t.a. books[1] for children.

(ii) *Transfer from i.t.a. to t.o.*
As has been explained earlier, teachers were urged not to change their methods of teaching reading when introducing i.t.a. into their classrooms, but it was necessary to suggest certain new techniques in connection with forming the characters of i.t.a. and the transfer stage from i.t.a. to t.o.

---

[1] A full description of the i.t.a. writing-system is given on pp. 93-111 of: Downing, J. A. (1965). *The Initial Teaching Alphabet Explained and Illustrated.* London: Cassell, and New York: Macmillan.

Research Report on the British Experiment with i.t.a.

The transition stage was of special concern to teachers. They were often anxious about this aspect, and it seemed very important not to make a child switch from i.t.a. to t.o. too early. It was pointed out that Pitman's design for transfer was based on the development, prior to the transition stage, of two skills: reading from minimal cues (the 'top coast-line' of the print) and the use of contextual clues to meaning. These were unlikely to be developed before a child could read at *Janet and John* Book IV stage or even the book following. Judgment of readiness for transfer should not be based solely on the book reached, but should be based more on the quality of the reading. In particular, it would be very important, it was suggested, to ensure that the child was reading from such a book in a meaningful way.

It was indicated that transfer from i.t.a. to t.o. should not be dramatic but that the child should be allowed to move over smoothly when he was ready. For this reason it seemed best not to emphasize the differences between i.t.a. and t.o., but to rely chiefly on the similarity of configurations as had been proposed by Pitman. Precise instructions for transfer materials were not given, but a number of alternatives were suggested. These alternatives were necessary in order to allow for differences in the overall 'philosophies' of the teachers. Some teachers gave the children the same book in t.o. as they had just read in i.t.a.; some went further back in the t.o. series; and others preferred to move to a different series in t.o. or to more individualized reading of t.o. books.

(iii) *Writing in* i.t.a. *and Transfer to Writing in* t.o.

A number of suggestions were made to deal with the unusual situation in respect of spelling in the experimental classes. In Britain, the Infants' teachers generally give priority to developing discovery and creativity and this applies to writing as well as to other first-hand experiences of the environment. Handwriting and spelling are relegated to a secondary position. At first, the Infants' teacher is pleased if children are able to write at all. Then, as the child's confidence and desire to write about his experiences grow, the teacher may begin to show him correct spellings, taking care to avoid damage to her pupil's motivation for free composition.

In the i.t.a. experiment, teachers were asked to maintain this aim as usual, to avoid inhibiting the child's creative writing, but it was pointed out that, when the stage of giving some spelling corrections was reached, certain special considerations would be necessary.

The First i.t.a. Experiment—Aims, Methodology and Design

Generally, one would select for correction words which are commonest in usage, but in the i.t.a. classes it would be necessary to select further from these more common words, those which had the same spelling in t.o. For example, buter could be corrected to butter, and kat to cat. It was proposed that spellings which were only i.t.a. conventions should not be corrected, to avoid focussing attention on i.t.a. spellings which would be different in t.o., e.g. ort should not be corrected to aut.

It was suggested that the transfer in writing should take place at an even more leisurely pace than in reading. More formal teaching of t.o. spelling should be postponed until after the child had begun the transfer in reading. A mixture of i.t.a. and t.o. might be anticipated for many months, and this should be tolerated to avoid inhibiting free composition. It was proposed that a useful method of teaching formal spelling would be one based on these children's experience of the more consistent representation of phonemes in i.t.a. For instance, at transfer the child could be shown that there is no character for the sound of ie in t.o., and that one common way of writing this sound is *ie* as in *die, pie, lie*. Subsequently the 'i-consonant-e letter-group' could be shown (e.g. *dine, pine, line*). Other spellings of this sound could then be postponed until later, but where it occurs in commonly-used, but irregularly-spelt words, the spelling could be taught earlier as an irregularity.

These were the only important suggestions on teaching methods given at these two-day courses. New teaching techniques were only suggested when the new characters and spelling rules of i.t.a. created some gap in existing common practices. But it must be recognized that, although the course was designed only to equip the teacher with essential information on i.t.a. itself, and to persuade teachers to preserve their existing teaching methods, it seems possible that teachers may unwittingly have been influenced by the course in other ways. In particular, it will be necessary to consider whether learning i.t.a. may have given these teachers greater insight into the nature of the child's task of learning to read. One further point should be noted in this description of the procedure of the experiment. Although refresher courses were provided for control classes they were not the same as those given to the i.t.a. classes. This will be discussed further when measures taken to control the 'Hawthorne Effect' are described.

(c) Preparation of Parents for the i.t.a. Experiment

When the first experimental i.t.a. and control t.o. classes began in 1961, one further preparatory measure had to be taken. The parents of the children who were to learn i.t.a. had to be prepared for this novel experiment. A pamphlet entitled *How Your Children Are Being Taught to Read with The Augmented Roman Alphabet*[1] described the purpose of the experiment and encouraged parents to accept the new writing-system as part of the normal educational scene. It contained a description of the alphabet so that parents could use it if they wished to write for their children. This pamphlet was distributed to parents with a covering letter from the L.E.A. Some headteachers held parents' meetings at which the Head of the Reading Research Unit gave a talk to explain the experiment. The large majority of parents accepted the experiment although many showed signs of misgiving. Only two or three cases are known of parents withdrawing their children from the experimental schools. The Experimenter's observation of the situation in 1961 and 1962 is that without these precautions, parental objections would probably have been too strong to have allowed the experimental classes to start.

However, these activities designed to gain the parents' acceptance of the i.t.a. experiment raise another problem of assessing the validity of the findings. These activities could not be matched in the control classes, e.g. no parents' pamphlet was available for parents of children learning with t.o.

(d) Testing of Subjects for Background Data and Matching

As early as possible after the children joined the experimental or control classes they were tested individually on Raven's Coloured Progressive Matrices and the Crichton Vocabulary Scale. These tests were administered by teachers, but not by the child's own class teacher. The teachers were given a special training course on the administration of these tests.

Information required for matching Experimental and Control Groups was obtained by questionnaire and in visits to the schools during the first year after the school joined the research project.

---

[1] DOWNING, J. A. (1961). This title was later changed to *How Your Children are Being Taught to Read with the Initial Teaching Alphabet*, revised edition 1964. (Reading Research Document No. 2). London: University of London Institute of Education.

The First i.t.a. Experiment—Aims, Methodology and Design

(e) Comparisons of i.t.a. Learning with t.o. Learning

The testing of reading has been by standardized tests, apart from the assessment of progress made by means of records of books read in the basic reading series. In the earlier part of the experiment, when the children in the experimental classes were learning to read with i.t.a., the standardized t.o. tests were transliterated into i.t.a. The i.t.a. versions of these tests were identical in every way with the t.o. test, apart from the use of the i.t.a. writing-system. Although putting the t.o. test into i.t.a. makes it impossible to draw conclusions, for example, about reading ages of subjects taking the i.t.a. test, it does provide a critical comparison between i.t.a. reading achievements and t.o. reading achievements in reading parallel samples of the English language in well-established test situations.

(f) Measures Taken to Control Hawthorne Effect

Another factor which should be considered in judging the results of this initial experiment is the contact which the Experimenter and his assistants have had with the teachers in the experimental and control classes respectively in the day-to-day administration of the experiment. It is important to note the extent and nature of these contacts between experimental and control class teachers and the experimenters, and to begin to form some judgment of the likely motivating effects on the teachers and children in each group. In this connection other interfering motivational factors should be considered, e.g. press and television publicity for i.t.a.:

(i) Contact between Research Team and Experimental and Control Groups

Contact between the research team and the Experimental and Control Groups has been by telephone, mail, visits of the Experimenter or assistants to schools, and at local meetings organized by the Experimenter in collaboration with L.E.A.s.

The telephone and mail communications have been largely the same for both experimental and control teachers—chiefly the business of organizing the testing programme. One point of difference which should be noted is that there was extra communication, mainly by mail, between the Experimenter and the experimental teachers on the question of materials in i.t.a. In the first year especially, but also in the second and third years of the initial experiment, there were often delays in getting i.t.a. materials to the schools and this caused additional contact between the Experimental Group and the Experimenter. Also the publication of i.t.a. books was spread

Research Report on the British Experiment with i.t.a.

over the first and second years, necessitating further communication between experimental schools and the Experimenter. Lists of new i.t.a. books were circulated every few months, and an emergency do-it-yourself scheme for making i.t.a. books was organized. Paste-over sheets with the i.t.a. text were duplicated centrally and distributed to the experimental schools for fixing over the original t.o. text. These additional contacts were unavoidable, but must be recognized in judging the results of the initial experiment.

School visiting may seem perhaps to be of greater importance. The policy of the Experimenter was to equalize the number of visits to experimental and control schools, but it seems likely that this policy has not been effective in several of the schools in this initial experiment. In the early part of the experiment, crises, especially over materials, often led to additional visits to experimental schools in order to help teachers to improvise materials or even to deliver books urgently needed for children who were making more rapid progress. Without these visits it seems certain that some experimental schools would have withdrawn from the research project because of these early problems.

(ii) *Other Visitors to the Research Classes*

Some of the experimental schools have also had visitors who were not members of the research team. In the initial experiment the public interest in the i.t.a. research which began to be aroused, or—mainly after the second year—had not been foreseen. It had not been agreed to exclude visitors because the demand had not been anticipated, and as a result some of the experimental schools had many visitors. This does not apply to all the schools using i.t.a., for some schools had relatively few outside visitors, but one may generalize with some certainty that some of the experimental schools had considerably more visitors than any of the control schools. Again, this probably was to be expected because visiting educators are interested in seeing the new experimental approach rather than the traditional approach, but it is a factor which must be borne in mind in weighing the evidence in this first i.t.a. experiment. It will be difficult to assess the influence of these additional outside visitors to the experimental schools, because there are likely to be *both negative and positive effects* arising from such visits. As soon as the problem of visitors began to appear serious, this variable was controlled rigorously in the second experiment with i.t.a. which was launched in September 1963.

The First i.t.a. Experiment—Aims, Methodology and Design

(iii) *Publicity for the Experimental Classes*

This seems to be an appropriate place to mention another interfering factor which should be taken into account in evaluating these experiments with i.t.a., namely the unusual publicity in the press and on television and radio for this new approach to the teaching of reading. Some publicity (generally not unfavourable to the experimental use of i.t.a.) appeared when the experiment was launched and there is no doubt that this was helpful in gaining acceptance for the experiment to take place at all. After the second year, however, the publicity in favour of i.t.a. began to increase, and it seems likely that this may have been positively motivating to teachers, parents and perhaps children in the Experimental Group. It may also have had a negative effect in the Control Group. It is possible, however, that there may have been a boomerang effect producing the opposite motivating effect in at least some teachers in both groups.

This publicity may have been largely unavoidable. Also, it must be admitted that the Experimenter's interim reports have to be included in considering 'publicity' effects. Interim reports of results from the i.t.a. experiments began to be issued in the second year in order to provide at least some objective basis for educational judgment as opposed to the anecdotal and even exaggerated accounts that were becoming current. Publicity, therefore, is a factor to be noted in any description of the conditions of the experiment.

(iv) *Meetings of Teachers in the Research Project*

Returning to the question of contact between the Experimenter and the two Groups—Experimental and Control—in the initial investigation, it seems especially important to take account of the local meetings of teachers in the research. Since i.t.a. was a highly novel approach, some features of which were a source of considerable misgiving to teachers and parents as well as to those concerned with administering the research, the Experimenter felt bound to keep a close watch on developments to safeguard the interests of the children. Therefore meetings of the teachers of the i.t.a. experimental classes were held as often as possible at first, in order to bring out in discussion any difficulties which they were experiencing. In the event, these difficulties turned out to be chiefly centred on such matters as the supply of i.t.a. materials, but no doubt teachers also learned to handle i.t.a. teaching more successfully through exchanging experiences. These meetings of the Experimental Group teachers were conducted by the Experimenter or an assistant and were generally held after school at a local centre. They lasted for about one to one and a half hours. In 1961-62, when there were teething-troubles in the administration of the experiment, the Experimental Group teachers had the opportunity of attending seven such meetings. In 1962-63 when the initial problems of materials began to be resolved it was not necessary to meet so frequently and only three meetings were held. Since then only two meetings each year have been provided.

In the design of this initial experiment it was recognized that although these meetings would be necessary for the teachers using i.t.a., at the same time they might increase the Hawthorne Effect in this group. It was proposed, therefore, that meetings should also be held for the teachers in the Control Group proper in an attempt to induce a similar increase in Hawthorne Effect in this group. It seems probable that these meetings of Control Group teachers have not been truly matched in quality with those of the teachers using i.t.a. The purpose was obviously different. The Experimenter and his assistants tried to show their concern for the teaching of reading in the control schools where t.o. was being employed as usual. Sometimes the research officer conducted the meeting alone, but often an outside speaker well known as an expert in Infant School teaching-methods was engaged to give an address followed by discussion. These Control Group meetings were sometimes held in the afternoon, and in some cases lasted longer than the Experimental Group meetings. There were on average two such meetings in each of the critical years of the research. Although it should be noted that these arrangements were not uniformly successful, it seems fair to make the generalization that a reasonable demonstration of interest in the normal t.o. work was provided. Inadequate finance for the research in the early stages made it impossible to make an objective assessment of teachers' motivation in the two groups.

CHAPTER III

Results of the First i.t.a. Experiment

IN previous interim reports on the results of the initial experiment with i.t.a. (e.g. Downing, 1964, 1965)[1, 2] caution in evaluating the preliminary findings has been urged consistently. This caution was necessary partly because this was a longitudinal study in mid-stream and partly because the procedure of matching experimental with control classes was incomplete.

The latter reason for postponing judgment no longer applies as far as the first i.t.a. experiment is concerned, because matching of Experimental and Control Groups is now as complete as it can be.

In order to render the i.t.a. and t.o. groups as comparable as possible, the schools were divided off into 'matched pairs'. The matching variables used, and the values that each variable could assume, were as follows:

Variable	Number of Values	Enumeration of Values
1. Urban/Rural Location	2	(*a*) Urban, (*b*) Rural
2. School Organization	2	(*a*) Infants only (*b*) Junior and Infants combined
3. School Size; Number of Infants on Roll	4	(*a*) 1-49, (*b*) 50-119, (*c*) 120-239, (*d*) 240 plus
4. Pupil/Teacher Ratio	4	(*a*) 10-20, (*b*) 21-30, (*c*) 31-40, (*d*) 41 plus
5. Amenities of the School Building (points on Morris' Scale)	3	(*a*) 1-8, (*b*) 9-13, (*c*) 14-17
6. Minimum age of Entry	4	(*a*) 3-3.11 (*b*) 4-4.5, (*c*) 4.6-4.11 (*d*) 5-5.5
7. Social Class (Fathers' Occupations—Registrar General's categories)	5+	(*a*) 2,2,3; (*b*) 2,3,3; (*c*) 3, 3, 3; (*d*) 3, 3, 4; (*e*) 3,4,4; etc.

[1] DOWNING, J. A. (1964). *The i.t.a. Reading Experiment*. London: Evans; and Chicago: Scott, Foresman.
[2] DOWNING, J. A. (1965). *The Initial Teaching Alphabet Explained and Illustrated*. London: Cassell, and New York: Macmillan.

Items 1, 2 and 3 are self-explanatory. Item 4 was calculated as the number of infants on roll, divided by the number of full-time teachers (of infants)—two 'half-time' teachers counting as one 'full-time' teacher. Average ratios for the school were used (rather than special averages for research classes) because:

(a) in many cases the research classes had not been formed when the matching was done, and

(b) the initial size of class during the early part of the year, especially in reception classes, was often considerably smaller than the overall average size of class.

The three-category assessment in respect of item 5 was based on criteria given by Morris. Morris' system of assessment is patently arbitrary. For example, there is no reason to think that having a hall is three times as valuable as having electric light. On the other hand, it does provide a crude basis for comparison, and it is fair to say that no better basis has yet been offered.

Item 6 was a means of reducing the risk of a significant variation in age between i.t.a. and t.o. populations in otherwise matched schools.

With regard to item 7, it should be noted that data relating to the research children were not obtainable at the time when the matched samples had to be agreed. In many cases, the children concerned had not yet entered school. Initial matching was therefore based partly on data relating to children who entered school the previous year or, for the September 1963 class, on teachers' estimates of the school population. The salient information was then classified according to the Registrar General's list. Where ambiguity occurred a general rule was adopted of applying the most likely interpretation. Thus 'engineer' was allocated to Class 3 unless additional information indicated that Class 2 or Class 1 was more appropriate. For purposes of matching, this information was summarized in terms of the 25th, 50th and 75th percentiles. Thus the first vector of numbers (2, 2, 3) signifies that the 25th and 50th percentiles both took the value Class 2, whereas the 75th percentile took the value Class 3 for a given school. Matching was in terms of these percentile points, e.g. between two (2, 2, 3) schools. It should be noted, however, that when the data relating to the critical hypotheses of these enquiries were analysed after the experiment, information concerning variable 7 was available for the research children, and was used in the study of their own backgrounds—as reported for each of the measures in this chapter.

Results of the First i.t.a. Experiment

A permutation of the first six items shows that $2 \times 2 \times 4 \times 4 \times 3 \times 4 = 768$ distinct categories of school are allowed for in this matching scheme. As the number of schools initially willing to participate was comparatively small, very few perfect matches could be achieved. It was therefore necessary to tolerate departures from the ideal requirement and to impose an order of priorities in allowing such departures. In the absence of any firm direction from existing research data, it was decided to adhere rigidly to items 1 and 2—so that rural schools were matched only with rural schools, and separately organized Infant Schools were matched only with separately organized Infant Schools, etc. A one-step departure was, however, allowed in respect of item 3—so that a school in the 1-49 category could be matched with a school in the 50-119 category, etc. Similarly, a one-step departure was allowed in respect of item 4. In all cases, however, the *absolute* discrepancy was kept as small as possible. Thus, if a school in the pupil/teacher ratio category of 21-30 were matched with another in the category 31-40 it might be the case that the first ratio equalled 29, and the other equalled 33. The absolute difference here is only 4 (33-29), notwithstanding the fact that the categories are different.

Because of the arbitrariness of item 5 (type of building) this matching variable was used only if there was still a choice existing after the matching requirements of items 1-4 had been satisfied. This meant that about half the matched schools ended up by being one category out, and just a few were two categories out (i.e. a type of building in the 0-8 category was matched with one in the 14-17 category).

With regard to item 6, this was not given a particularly high priority rating. But there happened to be enough uniformity among the schools to allow a good match to be made. Most schools fell within the same age category, and the remainder were rarely more than one category apart. Similar comments hold for item 7 except that, where there was a conflict between satisfying variable 5 and satisfying variable 7, variable 7 was given precedence.

The overall effect of this procedure was to secure the best match that could be obtained, having regard to the circumstances existing at the time, although many schools had to be rejected and the samples thereby made smaller because no matched partner could be found.

Within each pair of matched schools, steps were taken to *equalize sample sizes* so that the contribution of each member of the pair of schools to the total sample was the same. In this way biases due, for example, to a particularly good school contributing more results to one group than its matched pair in the other group, have been minimized. For each critical test of attainment, subjects were discarded by random procedure to equalize the contributions of each school (or class) in the matched experimental and control pair. Although this method of matching on school variables seemed likely to produce also a matching on some of the pupil variables, it was necessary to check the comparability of the samples on important pupil variables. Therefore, on each critical test reported in this chapter the background data for the children who actually took the test have been analysed to check whether there are any significant differences between the Experimental and Control Groups in respect of the following variables:

1. Age,
2. Sex,
3. Social Class (by fathers' occupations),
4. Score on Raven's Coloured Progressive Matrices,
5. Score on Crichton Vocabulary Scale.

In addition, the degree of success of the initial matching procedure on the following school variables was checked for significant differences in relation to the sample used on each of the tests:

6. Urban/Rural Location of School,
7. Type of School Organization (Infants only or Infants and Junior combined),
8. Size of School,
9. Pupil-Teacher Ratio at School,
10. Amenities of School Building (Points Score of School).

The numbers of children taking the different tests varied mainly because of children's absences, but sometimes a whole class missed a test through some mischance in the testing programme in the schools and this naturally has reduced the sizes of the samples. Sometimes tests were administered only to a sub-sample for reasons of economy.

The Experimental and Control Groups were found to be generally rather well equated on these pupil and school variables. Where the backgrounds of the Control and Experimental Groups differed significantly—as they did in a few cases—it was generally the *Control* Group that was favoured.

This means that in cases where i.t.a. results are superior, the extent of their superiority is likely to be somewhat underestimated. It will be noted in particular that matching in respect of amenities of the school building was often less than ideal. The reason for this is that an order of priorities had to be imposed with respect to matching procedures. This was so, because the schools initially willing to participate in the experiment were too heterogeneous to permit a really good match to be made on *all* the variables listed. Since the amenities (type of building) classification is generally admitted to be arbitrary, it was accorded the lowest priority rating. The schools were therefore paired off in the first instance with respect to the more important variables. But this left only a few degrees of freedom with which to secure a good match with respect to amenities of the school building. The final pairing off was reasonably satisfactory within any one pair of schools, but the overall differences (when cumulated over *all* pairs of schools) were unavoidably significant in some cases.

Wherever a significant difference at the five per cent. level exists between the Experimental and Control Groups on one of the background variables in respect of a particular set of data, this is reported along with the particular attainment test results which follow. If no difference is mentioned, this indicates that no statistically significant difference was found between the groups in respect of age, sex, social class, Raven's Coloured Progressive Matrices scores, Crichton Vocabulary Scale scores, and status in respect of the other variables listed above.[1]

It may be noted that this report deals with smaller numbers of subjects than did some earlier interim publications.[2] This is due mainly to the more rigorous matching procedure employed here. Also, only September entrants from both Experimental and Control Groups have been included in the critical tests of the hypotheses of the present study because of the important differences in educational treatment of January and April entrants which have been observed by the Experimenter in the course of the fieldwork.[3] These January and April entrants were only a comparatively small minority of the pupils in the experimental and control schools. Further reductions in the numbers of subjects have been caused through absences, removals, etc.

---

[1] Full details of the data on background variables in the two groups are provided in a separate publication, *The i.t.a. Symposium Technical Appendix*, available in duplicated form from the N.F.E.R., Slough, Bucks.

[2] It should also be noted that this present report is based on an analysis of the results which is different from those used in the earlier interim reports.

[3] On this point see also: (*a*) JINKS, P. C. (1964). 'An investigation into the effect of date of birth on subsequent school performance'. *Educational Research*, VI, 220-227; (*b*) PIDGEON, D. A., and DODDS, E. H. (1961). 'Length of schooling and its effect on performance in the junior school'. *Educational Research*, III, 214-221.

Research Report on the British Experiment with i.t.a.

Although the other main reason given for caution in earlier reports on the i.t.a. experiment—that this is a longitudinal study still in mid-stream—still applies to the more complex problem of the longer-term effects of i.t.a. in the transfer-of-learning to t.o., definite conclusions on the comparison of initial learning to read with i.t.a. and t.o. in the early stages before the i.t.a. subjects make the transition to t.o. may now be stated with confidence.

1. General Results related to Hypotheses

The questions and hypotheses listed in Chapter II will now be treated in turn in this presentation of the results of the first i.t.a. experiment.

Question I: Can children learn to read more easily with i.t.a. than they can with t.o.?

Hypothesis 1: Children in i.t.a. classes should make significantly more rapid progress through their basic reader series.

The progress of the children in the Experimental and Control Groups was carefully recorded by the teachers, who kept an individual record card for each child. The book reached in the *Janet and John* series at four points in the child's school career was noted at the end of the first year of school; at the beginning of the fifth term of school; at the end of the second year at school and at the end of the seventh term of school. Chief among the limitations of this method of measuring reading achievement is the wide variation in standards required by teachers before they permit their pupils to move on to the next book. The record card used in this experiment required the teacher to note the date on which the pupil *successfully* completed each book. Although it was recognized that the teachers' standards of judgment of successful completion of a book might vary, this method was employed to allow comparisons with data reported in the most recent careful examination of standards of reading in the British primary schools[1] in which this method of measurement played an important role.

All four of the analyses of children's progress through the basic reader series show (see Table E1 p. 56) that the Experimental Group using the i.t.a. edition made significantly more rapid progress, thus supporting the first hypothesis.

[1] MORRIS, J. M. (1959). *Reading in the Primary School.* N.F.E.R. Research Reports, No. 12. London: Newnes.

Results of the First i.t.a. Experiment

Examination of the background data of the samples of these four analyses reveals that matching was not perfect. Significant differences at of least the five per cent. level of confidence between Experimental and Control Groups were found as follows:

After 1 *year:*
the i.t.a. Experimental Group was younger;
the i.t.a. Experimental Group pupils were more often in larger classes;
the i.t.a. Experimental Group pupils were more often in school buildings lacking in certain amenities.

After 1⅓ *years:*
the i.t.a. Experimental Group pupils were more often in larger classes;
the i.t.a. Experimental Group pupils were more often in school buildings lacking in certain amenities.

After 2 *years:*
the i.t.a. Experimental Group contained more boys and fewer girls;
the i.t.a. Experimental Group pupils were more often in school buildings lacking in certain amenities.

After 2⅓ *years:*
the i.t.a. Experimental Group pupils were more often in school buildings lacking in certain amenities.

All of these significant differences between the Experimental Group and the Control Group seem to have favoured the latter. Thus the superior rate of progress of the Experimental Group was achieved in spite of a degree of bias favourable to the Control Group.

Hypothesis 2: Pupils learning to read with i.t.a. should achieve significantly higher scores on reading tests in which lower-order decoding skills have an especially important role to play.

The Schonell Graded Word Reading Test[1] appears to be fairly well suited for a test of this hypothesis. It consists of a list of 100 words. The child is credited with one point in score for each word read and pronounced correctly. Schonell did not design the test specifically to measure what has been termed above 'lower-order de-

---

[1] SCHONELL, F. V., and SCHONELL, F. E. (1949). *Graded Word Reading Test.* Edinburgh: Oliver & Boyd.

coding ability', but since there are no contextual clues in such a word list it seems to place a premium on decoding ability in *very young* children who are unlikely to have learned many wholeword print configurations. Although the majority of schools in the experiment began with a look-say approach, as is normal in British schools, it was noted in the pilot classes that a few children seemed to develop phonic analysis and synthesis skills spontaneously. Also, teachers commented that their i.t.a. pupils appeared to show readiness for phonics somewhat earlier than is usual when t.o. is used. Certainly, such phonic decoding ability will increase the score of children who possess it relative to those who depend on identification of whole-word shapes. Therefore, to test this second hypothesis, children in i.t.a. classes were tested on an i.t.a. version of the Schonell test and their attainments compared with those pupils in the t.o. classes tested in t.o. All conditions besides the orthography were held constant (e.g. words, size of print, testing, environment, etc.). The Schonell test was administered in i.t.a. and t.o. to all the Experimental and Control Groups respectively at the end of the first school year, and at the commencement of the fifth term. Table E2 (p. 00) summarizes the results of the administration of the two tests.

Data on the backgrounds of the samples for each of the above two analyses show again that matching of the Experimental and Control Groups failed to some extent. The following significant differences between the two groups occurred:

After 1 *year:*
    the i.t.a. Experimental Group was younger;
    the i.t.a. Experimental Group pupils were more often in larger classes;
    the i.t.a. Experimental Group pupils were more often in school buildings lacking in certain amenities.

After $1\frac{1}{3}$ *years:*
    the i.t.a. Experimental Group was younger;
    the i.t.a. Experimental Group had fewer pupils in classes with school buildings superior in certain amenities.

Again these significant differences in the background data of the two groups appear to have favoured the Control Group. Thus the superior test scores of the i.t.a. Experimental Group have been achieved in spite of a degree of bias favouring the t.o. Control Group.

Results of the First i.t.a. Experiment

If the traditional alphabet and spelling of English is shown to be an important cause of difficulty in decoding, then it would be anticipated that such difficulty might frustrate children's attempts to read continuous English prose in terms of accuracy, speed and comprehension. To study further such differential effects of i.t.a. and t.o. on the development of reading skills, the Neale Analysis of Reading Ability[1] was applied just before the middle of the fifth term. This is a comprehensive reading test consisting of six passages of English narrative prose. The test provides measures of accuracy, speed, and comprehension. It should be noted, however, that these measures are not independent. For example, the accuracy level sets an upper limit on the comprehension score. It is important also to recognize the nature of the comprehension measure. The comprehension score is obtained by scoring children's answers to the passages they have read *orally*. It should be noted, too, that the administrator is permitted to supply words which the child has been unable to read for himself, and that the test terminates when a child makes sixteen or more errors in any of the first five tests. The pupils in the t.o. Control Group were given the standard t.o. edition of Form C of the Neale Test, while the i.t.a. Experimental Group took the identical test except for its being transliterated into i.t.a. Owing to the time and level of skill needed to administer the Neale test, only a sub-sample of the Experimental and Control Groups could be tested. All three measures of the Neale Test (Accuracy, Rate or Speed of Reading, and Comprehension) were used, and the results are shown in Tables E3, E4, and E5 (pp. 57-58).

The i.t.a. Experimental Group achieved significantly superior scores on all three of these measures. Although these sub-samples were otherwise well matched, data on their backgrounds show that the pupils in the Experimental Group were younger and that the Experimental Group had fewer pupils in school buildings superior in certain amenities.

These two differences seem likely to have given an advantage to the Control Group and therefore it may be said that the Experimental Group achieved superior scores in accuracy, speed and comprehension in spite of a degree of bias favourable to the Control Group in these two respects.

---

[1] NEALE, M. D. (1958). *Neale Analysis of Reading Ability* (three parallel forms—A, B and C). London: Macmillan.

Research Report on the British Experiment with i.t.a.

Question II: Can pupils transfer their training in reading in i.t.a. to reading in t.o.?

Hypothesis 3: In i.t.a. *classes, reading achievements in* t.o. *should not be inferior to previous achievements in* i.t.a. *once fluency in* i.t.a. *has been established.*

Towards the middle of the fifth term, Form C of the Neale Analysis of Reading Ability was administered to a sub-sample of the Experimental Group. This form was printed in i.t.a. One month later in the test programme, Form A of the Neale Analysis, this time *in t.o.*, was given to the i.t.a. group. The criterion test of hypothesis 3 was a comparison of the Experimental Group's i.t.a. scores on Form C with this same group's t.o. scores on Form A. The results from those children who were present for both tests were used. The data are shown in Tables E6, E7, and E8 (p. 00).

Hypothesis 3 appears to be supported in respect of only one of the three measures. The t.o. scores for speed were significantly superior to the i.t.a. scores for speed achieved by these same Experimental Group children one month earlier. On accuracy and comprehension there was a significant falling off when the i.t.a. group was tested in t.o. instead of i.t.a. It must be noted, however, that approximately two-thirds of the children had not been transferred to reading t.o. books by their teachers when Neale A in t.o. was administered.

As this test of the hypothesis does not take account of the proviso 'once fluency in i.t.a. has been established', a further comparison of the Neale A t.o. data with the Neale C i.t.a. data was made utilizing only the results of children who had been transferred from i.t.a. to t.o. reading materials by their teachers at least six weeks prior to the administration of Neale A in t.o. Tables E9, E10, and E11 (pp. 60-61) show the results of this further analysis of the data on accuracy, speed and comprehension respectively. The children referred to in these three tables are the same pupils for both tests.

Even those i.t.a. pupils who presumably were considered ready for transfer to t.o. by their teachers lost ground in reading accuracy. Also the better i.t.a. comprehension scores of this group suffered when the test was in t.o. Thus hypothesis 3 is not supported in respect of reading accuracy and reading comprehension.

Hypothesis 3 was supported, however, in respect of the speed of reading. This applies both to the results from the whole Experi-

Results of the First i.t.a. Experiment

mental Group sub-sample and to the results from the 152 subjects transferred to t.o. books by their teachers.

A later test provided further evidence in respect of hypothesis 3. The Schonell Graded Word Reading Test was administered to the Experimental Group in t.o. at the beginning of the third school year. The same test had been given to this group previously at the beginning of the fifth term, that is, more than half a school year earlier. The results of this test in i.t.a. and re-test in t.o. of the same subjects are shown in Table E12.

These results indicate that the i.t.a. group had t.o. scores at the beginning of the third year which were significantly inferior to what they had achieved on the i.t.a. version of the same test more than half a school year earlier. Thus the i.t.a. group's t.o. score on the second test represents no progress and even a regression in comparison to their i.t.a. score over half a year earlier.

However, again, this cannot be regarded as a valid test of hypothesis 3 because only 52·2 per cent. of these Experimental Group subjects had as yet been transferred to t.o. books by their teachers. Therefore, the results from 135 subjects, who had been tested on Schonell's Graded Word Reading Test in i.t.a. after one and one-third years and who had been re-tested in t.o. at the start of the third school year, were selected for special study, because these pupils had been transferred to t.o. reading books at least four months prior to the t.o. test. Their results are shown in Table E13 (p. 62).

The results from these superior pupils in the Experimental Group led to the rejection of hypothesis 3 in respect of reading as measured by the Schonell Graded Word Reading Test, since these pupils could read fewer test words in t.o. than they could read more than half a school year earlier on the i.t.a. version of the same test.

To investigate which words were more difficult for these 135 children to read in t.o. their errors on the first 50 words of Schonell's Graded Word Reading Test were analysed with the results shown in Table E14. Although the test was administered in t.o., Table E14 (p. 63) also shows the i.t.a. spelling of the words in order to provide some guide as to the degree of similarity between the i.t.a. and t.o. stimuli.

It is convenient to take the words in Schonell's order of difficulty, but to deal with them in groups of 10. Within these groups the more difficult words can then be noted. For example, there were three

Research Report on the British Experiment with i.t.a.

words in the first group of 10 which all 135 subjects read correctly in t.o. Two of these, *milk* and *egg* are spelled in precisely the same way in i.t.a. and t.o. The other word always read correctly was *little* in which the first five letters remain the same in t.o. as they were in i.t.a., the only difference being the addition of the final letter *e*. The two words with the largest number of errors in the first group were *school* and *playing*. These clearly are the two words among the first 10 which change most in the transition from i.t.a. to t.o. In the next group of 10 words the two with the least number of errors are *clock* and *summer*, which again are words which contain no significant changes from i.t.a. to t.o. spelling. The two words with most errors, *light* and *people*, are also words with major differences in the i.t.a. and t.o. stimuli for the same responses.

In words numbers 21-30, *shepherd* and *sandwich* have the fewest errors and these are very similar though not identical in i.t.a. and t.o. In this group the outstandingly difficult words were *postage* and *island*. *Postage* is one of the words in this group which differs considerably in its i.t.a. and t.o. forms. *Island*, however, seems to differ rather little in its general configuration. However, it is perhaps notable that the t.o. form contains the stimulus *s* which now requires a different response from the one formerly learned in i.t.a. It is perhaps also important that this difficulty occurs near the beginning of the word.

The design for transfer in i.t.a. is based on its similarity to the t.o. whole-word configuration, especially in respect of the top half of the line of print. By inspection, the word which, in the first group of 10 words, has a t.o. configuration least like its i.t.a. configuration is *school*. This was, in fact, the most difficult word to read in t.o. in that group. In the next 10 words, the t.o. configuration which is most unlike its i.t.a. configuration is *light*. This again was one of the most difficult in this group. In the next group (21-30) there is no word with an outstanding change in configuration, but two words, *postage* and *island*, did produce a markedly greater number of errors. In the fourth group, two words had major changes in their t.o. configurations, *gnome* and *nephew*, but they did not produce the greatest number of errors. *Canary*, with highly similar i.t.a. and t.o. configurations, proved to be the most difficult word in this group for these children making the transition from i.t.a. to t.o. In the final group the two most difficult words, *orchestra* and *knowledge*, do have important differences in their i.t.a. and t.o. configurations.

Results of the First i.t.a. Experiment

The use of the Schonell test's list of single words isolates the word-recognition aspect of transfer from i.t.a. forms to t.o. forms and seems very appropriate for this purpose. However, in the real-life reading situation contextual clues have an important role and, therefore, a test such as the Neale Analysis with its passages of continuous prose, is necessary to judge i.t.a.'s effectiveness as a transitional system under normal classroom conditions. The errors made by the 152 Experimental Group subjects on the Neale test Form A which was administered in t.o. in the middle of the second school year were tabulated with the result presented in Table E15 (pp. 64-65).

In the first passage one word caused more than twice as many errors as any other word. This was *Now* (nou). Its t.o. form differs from its i.t.a. form in several ways. In t.o. *Now* has a new capital letter and this alters the configuration of the word. Other capital letters in words of this first passage do not appear to be associated with special difficulty. The vowel phoneme in *Now* is also represented in t.o. by a different symbol, *ow* instead of ou, but this does not seem to be a very significant change from the configurational point of view. If children were using an analytical approach, however, the t.o. letters *o* and *w* would be misleading as these stimuli were associated with different responses in i.t.a. The word *house* (hous) only produced two errors, but the vowel phoneme which it has in common with *Now* is written *ou* in t.o. which is closer in form to i.t.a.'s ou. A complicating factor here is that *house* is the final word while *Now* is the first word in a sentence.

In the second passage the outstandingly difficult item was *the centre* (the senter). It produced 82 errors. The next most fruitful source of errors was *frightened* (frietend) with 51, and next came three items with a similar level of difficulty, *to safety* (tω sæfty)—41 errors; *returned* (returnd)—39 errors; *wandered* (wonderd)—37 errors. All of these items except one, *frightened* (frietend), appear to have very similar configurations in t.o. to their i.t.a. counterparts. One of these difficult words, *returned* (returnd) has not only highly similar i.t.a. and t.o. configurations, but also appears to have no seriously misleading detail in its t.o. spelling. *Centre* does have in initial position in the t.o. form, the t.o. letter *c* which in i.t.a. was associated with a different phoneme. In *wandered* (wonderd) the first vowel phoneme is represented in t.o. by a letter which had a different significance in i.t.a.

Research Report on the British Experiment with i.t.a.

In the third passage the most difficult items were:
1. *enabled* (enæbld)—87 errors.
2. *Tess to regain* (tess tω regæn)—85 errors.
3. *that brief* (ʃhat breef)—84 errors.
4. *future work* (fuetuer wurk)—81 errors.

In all four items the configurations of the t.o. and i.t.a. forms seem highly similar, but the details contain misleading elements which are likely to cause errors to children making an analytical approach rather than a configurational one. The *a* in *enabled* has a different value in t.o. to what it had in i.t.a. The *ie* in *brief* is close to i.t.a.'s ie with again a different value. The letters *or* in *work* represent the vowel sound with r common to pork, cork, fork in i.t.a., and most English children are likely to be misled by the t.o. spelling *work* into reading it as '*walk*'.

Returning to the study of the test scores of the Experimental Group in t.o. as compared with their earlier scores in i.t.a., it should be noted that no corresponding setback or even a plateau is discernable in the Control Group's progress through the same series of tests.

In order to see if there is any recovery from this setback in the Experimental Group as the children become more experienced in reading t.o., the results of the 171 subjects who were tested on the Neale test on all three occasions when it was administered, including the use of Form B in t.o. at the end of the third school year, were analysed separately. These results are shown in Tables E16, E17 and E18 (p. 66).

There is obviously a recovery in the scores of the i.t.a. Experimental Group in the sense that, although the t.o. accuracy and comprehension scores were, at the middle of the second school year, inferior to what they had been a month earlier in i.t.a., by the end of the third school year the t.o. scores are very superior to what they were in i.t.a. one-and-a-half school years earlier. However, in terms of the degree of superiority of the i.t.a. group over the t.o. group it seems less certain that there has been a recovery. In i.t.a. the accuracy scores of the Experimental Group taken as a whole had been almost double the t.o. scores of the Control Group, whereas by the end of the third year the mean t.o. scores of the Experimental Group as a whole and the Control Group were 38·97 and 31·66 respectively. This represents, of course, a significant degree of superiority in the i.t.a. group, equivalent to a gain of approximately six months in reading age, but the earlier superiority would, in t.o., have been equivalent to a lead of ten months in reading age.

Results of the First i.t.a. Experiment

Question III: After the whole process of beginning with i.t.a. and transferring to t.o., are reading attainments in t.o. superior to what they would have been without the intervention of i.t.a.?

Hypothesis 4: Pupils who have first learned to read with i.t.a. and then made the transition to t.o. should read the latter with significantly greater accuracy, speed and comprehension than pupils who have not used i.t.a. in the beginning.

From the middle of the fifth term the Experimental Group was tested *only in t.o.* to provide data for testing hypothesis 4.

The first criterion test was applied in the second half of the fifth term, Neale Analysis Form A in t.o. being administered to sub-samples of the Experimental and Control Groups. Summaries of the results are shown in Tables E19, E20 and E21 (p. 67).

Although the two groups were quite well matched, two differences appear to have existed which somewhat favoured the Control Group. The Experimental Group pupils were more often younger and accommodated in school buildings lacking in certain amenities.

Although the Experimental Group appears to have had superior scores on all three measures in this first test of t.o. reading attainment, in no case is the improvement statistically significant at the five per cent. level. Therefore, at this stage—halfway through the second year—hypothesis 4 is not supported. It should be noted, however, that about two-thirds of the pupils in the i.t.a. Experimental Group were still using i.t.a. materials and had not been transferred to t.o. books by their teachers.

A second test of hypothesis 4 was provided by administering the standard t.o. edition of the Schonell Graded Word Reading Test to both groups in the middle of the seventh term. The results are summarized in Table E22 (p. 68). The two significant differences found in the backgrounds of the subjects of the two groups both favoured the Control Group. It contained a larger proportion of girls and more pupils in school buildings superior in certain amenities.

The results of the Schonell test administered at the beginning of the third school year seem to support hypothesis 4 since the Experimental Group which had begun with i.t.a. now achieved *t.o. scores* superior to those of the Control Group which had been using t.o. from the very beginning.

The third test of hypothesis 4 was made by administering the Neale Analysis of Reading Ability Form B in t.o. to sub-samples from both Experimental and Control Groups at the end of the third school year. The results are summarized in Tables E23, E24 and

E25 (pp. 68-69). The groups appear to be well matched except that again the Control Group sub-sample had the advantage of containing more pupils in superior school buildings.

All three measures on this t.o. test seem to provide support for hypothesis 4. By the end of the third year the i.t.a. group achieved scores for accuracy, speed and comprehension in reading which were significantly superior to the t.o. scores obtained by the Control Group which had been using t.o. from the outset. These results may be contrasted with those obtained from the earlier application of Neale Form A in t.o. (after one and a half school years) when no significant differences were found between the t.o. scores of the Experimental and Control Groups.

Hypothesis 4 was tested in a fourth way on still another type of reading test. This was the Standish N.S. 45 Test[1]. This is a silent reading comprehension test originally designed for children at the beginning of the Junior School (ages 7 plus). In this experiment it was used at a slightly earlier stage. All pupils in the Experimental and Control Groups were given the Standish test in t.o. at the end of their Infant School careers. Some of these pupils had then been at school for only two years, but others had been at school for three years. The results for the two-year-taught and three-year-taught children are presented separately in Table E26 (p. 69).

In the two-year-taught groups there was a trend for t.o. pupils to be superior to the i.t.a. pupils. In the three-year-taught groups, this trend was reversed. But in neither case was the difference statistically significant at the five per cent. level. Among the two-year-taught pupils the i.t.a. group contained more pupils in larger schools. Among the three-year-taught pupils the t.o. group had an advantage in respect of amenities of the school building. These two differences were statistically significant.

Question IV: Will children's written compositions be more fluent with the simpler i.t.a. code for speech? (i.e. will the gap between their spoken and written vocabularies be narrowed?)

Hypothesis 5: The written compositions of i.t.a. pupils should be longer than those of children who begin reading in t.o.

Hypothesis 6: The written vocabulary of i.t.a. pupils should be more extensive than that of their t.o. counterparts.

A normal sample of one week's written work was obtained from an experimental group of 54 children who had begun with i.t.a. and

[1] Reading Test: Form N.S.45, by E. J. Standish, B.Sc. (N.F.E.R., unpublished).

Results of the First i.t.a. Experiment

a control group of 54 children who had started on t.o. The written work was collected during these children's seventh term at school, by which time the majority of i.t.a. children had made the transfer from i.t.a. to t.o. in their reading. The children came from schools in the geographical county of Staffordshire. The examination of hypotheses 5 and 6 was made in a subsidiary investigation of subsamples from the main experiment. The complete matching procedure outlined earlier could not be followed here. The two groups were matched on age, sex, social class (based on fathers' occupations), and score on Raven's Coloured Progressive Matrices. No information was obtained on the other background variables in respect of this test of hypotheses 5 and 6.[1]

The week's written work was not specially prepared or selected by the teacher. It was either collected without warning at the end of the week by the headteacher, or the Experimenter picked a week at random from a collection of a complete half-term's work. The criterion for testing hypothesis 5 was a simple count of the total number of words used in one week by each of the 108 pupils. The results are shown in Table E27 (p. 70). This total was then broken down to yield a 'net' vocabulary size (consisting of the total number of different words used) plus repetitions.[2] Since the children made extensive use of the basic vocabulary determined by Edwards and Gibbon[3], the 250 most popular words on their list were discounted to show how many 'more advanced' words remained. This meant that for each child a 2×2 contingency table was compiled to show (*a*) net basic vocabulary, (*b*) repetitions of basic vocabulary words, (*c*) net 'more advanced' vocabulary, and (*d*) repetitions of more advanced vocabulary words. The measures (*a*) and (*c*) provide a test of hypothesis 6.

A study of heterogeneity of individual results was carried out,

---

[1] More information related to hypotheses 5 and 6 will be published in the February 1967 issue of *Educational Research*, 'The Effects of the Initial Teaching Alphabet (i.t.a.) on Young Children's Written Composition', by the present author, together with Thomas Fyfe and Michael Lyon.

[2] While in general it may be questioned whether repetition is necessarily a valid criterion of quality of composition, it is generally recognized that sheer quantity in actual practice indicates greater fluency in composition in the early years of the Primary School, although, of course, this would not be true of writing, for example, at the Grammar School level.

[3] EDWARDS, R. F. A., and GIBBON, V. (1964). *Words Your Children Use*. London: Burke.

using a statistical method adapted from Snedecor[1] and Cochran[2]. This procedure justified averaging over individuals *within* schools, but not over sets of schools—because the t.o. and i.t.a. schools all differed significantly among themselves (p. < ·001 in both cases, using a variant of Cochran's strengthened chi-square test).

In the case of the t.o. group, five schools were used (involving 15, 8, 10, 14 and 7 children). In the case of the i.t.a. group, four schools were used (involving 15, 15, 8 and 16 children). These discrepancies were necessary in order to satisfy the matching criteria mentioned earlier. But the statistical analysis showed that school differences were too large to be discounted. Instead of pooling the results of the two sets of schools, Table E27, therefore, shows the *mean* performance per child for each of the nine schools in question.

By inspection, it can be seen that the t.o. schools are considerably more heterogeneous than the i.t.a. schools. After allowing for this, however, it remains true that there is a clear tendency for i.t.a. to give superior results. Even if *all* the t.o. schools were up to the standard of the best t.o. school in the set (School 1), the i.t.a. schools would still be significantly better with respect to overall word-count and total incidence of 'more advanced' words. Significance tests do not add much to the picture set out in Table E27, but an adaption of Cochran's strengthened chi-square test shows i.t.a. to be significantly better (p. < ·001) than t.o. on all the measures discussed.

It is, of course, an open question whether these differences are due to uncontrolled factors. It was noticeable, for example, that different schools submitted writings with different recurring *themes* (visits to zoo, visits to sea, etc.). Presumably some themes give rise to higher word-counts and to larger numbers of 'advanced' words than do others. All that can be said on this score is that a subjective examination of the writing samples did *not* give the impression that the i.t.a. schools were advantageously placed. The overall impression (supported by syntactic analyses and analyses of content) is that the i.t.a. children were genuinely superior in their written composition work. Some examples of i.t.a. composition work have been published previously.[3]

---

[1] SNEDECOR, G. W. (1956). *Statistical Methods*. Iowa: Iowa State College Press.

[2] COCHRAN, W. G. (1954). 'Some Methods of Strengthening the Common χ^2 Tests'. *Biometrics*, 10, 417-451.

[3] DOWNING, J. A. (1964). *Examples of Children's Creative Writing from Schools using* i.t.a. (Reading Research Document No. 4). London: University of London Institute of Education.

Results of the First i.t.a. Experiment

Question V: How will children's later attainments in t.o. spelling be influenced by their earlier experiences of reading and writing the different spellings of i.t.a.?

Hypothesis 7: Spelling attainments in t.o. after the transition stage should be superior in classes where i.t.a. was used for the beginning stage.

As a criterion test for hypothesis 7, Schonell's Graded Word Spelling Test was applied twice:

Form A: administered individually in the middle of the third school year;

Form B: administered as a group test in the middle of the fourth school year.

Only correct t.o. spellings were credited in both groups. Correct i.t.a. spellings which were incorrect in t.o. were marked 'wrong' in both groups. The results for these two tests are presented in Table E28 (p. 71).

The results of both tests indicate that the Experimental Group pupils who originally learned to read and write with i.t.a. have t.o. spelling attainments which are superior after the transfer to those of the Control Group children who have been reading and writing with t.o. from the very beginning. However, only on the second spelling test does the difference reach the five per cent. level of statistical significance. Thus hypothesis 7 is supported by the evidence from these tests.

On the first spelling test the Control Group appears to have been favoured in terms of pupil-teacher ratio. On the second spelling test the Control Group was again favoured in terms of the school buildings in which its pupils were accommodated.

2. Results for Low Achieving, Average Achieving, and High Achieving Segments of the Experimental and Control Groups

Much of the discussion surrounding the question of the introduction of proposed educational innovations centres around two issues:

(i) Is the new technique really necessary for those who already achieve well with existing methods? For example, it is frequently commented that 'the bright children learn anyway'.

(ii) Will the new technique help teachers with those cases which are difficult to teach under existing methods? For example, 'the acid test is—will it help the slow-learners?' is another comment often heard. To aid judgment on these issues in regard to the use of i.t.a. for beginning reading and writing, special analyses have been made

Research Report on the British Experiment with i.t.a.

of the data reported in the previous section of this chapter. The graphs relating to this section (pp. 73-90) show for each test what were the differences between the i.t.a. and t.o. groups' results for varying levels of achievement.

More precisely the graphs show how i.t.a. and t.o. results compare for ten ranges of achievement.

The ranges were established by first ranking the scores in each group and then dividing them into ten equal 'Achievements Categories', the first category representing the bottom ten per cent. of the scores, the second category the next ten per cent., and so on.

Average scores were then computed for each Achievement Category, and by this means a comparison of i.t.a. and t.o. results for each category was made possible.

By joining up the points representing the average scores, curves could be obtained and inferences made concerning, for example, any general trends observed.

Although the graphs were produced in terms of average scores for ten ranges of achievement, the comment which follows has in mind three groupings of practical concern to teachers judging the effects of i.t.a.:

(*a*) The Low Achievers
(Scores falling within the lowest three Achievement Categories)
(*b*) The Middle Achievers
(Scores falling within the middle four Achievement Categories)
(*c*) The High Achievers
(Scores falling within the highest three Achievement Categories)

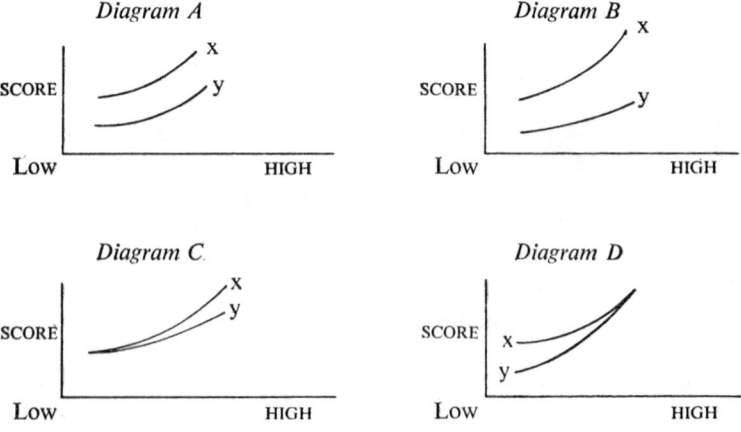

Results of the First i.t.a. Experiment

Some typical kinds of results are shown in Diagrams A-D (p. 44). Of necessity, all graphs rise from left to right. But their relative locations can be informative. In Diagram A, for example, the two graphs rise in parallel indicating that all subjects (from the worst to the best) benefit by the same constant amount from method X. In Diagram B, the magnitude of the difference increases from left to right, indicating that High Achievers benefit more from method X than do Low Achievers. This type of image suggests a proportional, rather than a constant-increment benefit from method X. In Diagram C, the curves overlap on the left of the graph, but separate towards the right. This implies that method X does nothing to help the Low Achievers. Diagram D shows the converse situation in which method X is helpful to Low Achievers, but of little use to High Achievers (who can manage just as well with method Y).

It is of some interest to note that uninformed speculation about i.t.a. has sometimes favoured the Diagram C image, and sometimes the Diagram D image. In other words, it has sometimes been conjectured that i.t.a. would be of special value to the slow learner, but of little use to the brighter child who would 'learn anyway'. Conversely, it has been suggested that brighter children might benefit more because they are better able to comprehend and exploit the regularities implicit in the simplified i.t.a. system.

Inspection of the graphs relating to the ranges of achievement suggests:

(*a*) that the High Achievers (scores falling in the three highest Achievement Categories) in the i.t.a. group were superior to the High Achievers in the t.o. group on most tests. Generally among the High Achievers, the i.t.a. group demonstrated a greater degree of superiority over t.o. pupils than was found among the Middle and Low Achievers.

(*b*) that Middle Achievers taught by i.t.a., though not as markedly superior to t.o. pupils as among High Achievers, nevertheless showed an important degree of superiority over the t.o. pupils in the Control Group.

(*c*) that among the Low Achievers (scores falling in the three lowest Achievement Categories) on the earliest tests, little or no measurable differences existed between the scores of the i.t.a. and t.o. groups. However, later tests indicate that the i.t.a. Low Achievers became superior to their t.o. counterparts, but that this was not true of the poorest students of all, represented by the lowest ten per cent. of the samples. During the time when i.t.a. subjects were being tested in i.t.a. (i.e. the first $1\frac{1}{2}$ years) no difference was found between their scores and those of the t.o. subjects in this lowest Achievement Category of all.

When t.o. testing began in the middle of the second school year, the Low Achievers (three lowest Achievement Categories) of the i.t.a. group at first fell behind the t.o. group, but later at the end of the third year, the i.t.a. Low Achievers became generally superior to the t.o. Low Achievers on tests of t.o. reading and spelling attainments. The superior scores of the Low Achievers in the i.t.a. group on the spelling tests and on the Standish N.S.45 Test of the three-year-taught pupils seem worthy of note.

The above statements are concerned with trends observed by inspection of the graphs. A detailed discussion of the data shown in them is being published elsewhere.[1]

3. Results of Check on Effectiveness of Attempts to Stimulate Hawthorne Effect in the Control Group

The efforts made by the Experimenter to stimulate the degree of Hawthorne Effect in the Control Group which might be expected to have been created in the Experimental Group have been described in Chapter II. To test the effectiveness of these procedures, the reading standards in the control schools were measured before and after the commencement of the experiment. The Standish N.S. 45 Test of silent reading comprehension was administered at the end of the final year of the Infants School. Two groups of children were compared; (i) those pupils who had been in the school before the research project began and whose teachers had not participated in the procedures designed to enhance Hawthorne Effect, (ii) the pupils of the Control Group proper in the research project whose teachers had participated in the special procedures designed to enhance Hawthorne Effect. *All* entrants were included in this test, i.e. January and April entrants as well as September entrants. In Table E29 (p. 00) the results are shown from thirty of the control schools. Twelve schools used in the Control Group are not included because eleven joined the research project only in 1963 and, therefore, it was too early to test control classes properly. The other school, through error, had not carried out the test on the special control class at the appropriate time.

In the large majority of cases there was no significant difference between the results for the pre-research pupils and the results for

[1] DOWNING, J. A. (1967). *Evaluating the Initial Teaching Alphabet.* London: Cassell.

the pupils whose teachers participated in the research project with the special attempts to enhance factors believed to cause Hawthorne Effect. In four schools the results deteriorated after the period when Hawthorne Effects should have been operating, and in only three schools did standards improve. These results indicate that in most of the schools standards did not change significantly and therefore, there is no evidence of Hawthorne Effect in the Control Group. It should be recognized, however, that the measures used may have been inadequate to detect any such effect.[1]

---

[1] A more detailed discussion of the Hawthorne Effect in connection with the present research is contained in: DOWNING, J. A. (1967). *Evaluating the Initial Teaching Alphabet.* London: Cassell. The significance of Hawthorne Effect in educational research is not known. It is currently under investigation in America, e.g. COOK, D. L. (1964). 'The Hawthorne Effect and reading research'. In: FIGUREL, J. A., ed. *Improvement of Reading Through Classroom Practice.* Newark, Delaware: International Reading Association.

CHAPTER IV

Conclusions

METHODOLOGICAL problems arising from the need to satisfy the often conflicting demands on the one hand, of maintaining realistic school conditions and, on the other, of gaining rigorous scientific control of the many complex variables, made the first i.t.a. experiment difficult to plan and conduct, and, finally, its results difficult to evaluate. The most frequently raised question about the validity of the first i.t.a experiment's results was the possibility of Hawthorne Effect. A detailed discussion of this problem of Hawthorne Effect in reading research is being published elsewhere.[1] Briefly, in this first i.t.a. experiment, the method of controlling this factor was to ensure that any likely causes of Hawthorne Effect in the Experimental Group were also reproduced in the Control Group. The empirical check on Hawthorne Effect in the latter group, however, showed no evidence of such effect. In the second i.t.a. experiment,[2] possible causes of this effect seem likely to have been more rigorously equated and reduced to a minimum, but the results of the comparison of i.t.a. and t.o. learning appear to be, so far, similar to those in the first i.t.a. experiment.

The little evidence available on this problem from the two experiments suggests that the importance of a Hawthorne Effect in the i.t.a. research has been exaggerated. Indeed, its absence in the Control Group of the first experiment despite deliberate efforts to stimulate Hawthorne Effect in it, raises doubts as to whether this concept can validly be taken over from industrial experiments to educational ones—at least when such young children are the subjects.

Where it has been difficult to equate the treatment or composition of the Experimental and Control Groups in the two experiments the difference has tended to favour the Control Group (e.g. in the supply of books in both experiments), and as the superior attainments have generally been found in the Experimental Group, this suggests that this superiority of i.t.a. has tended to be underestimated in this research.

[1] DOWNING, J. A. (1967). *Evaluating the Initial Teaching Alphabet*. London: Cassell.
[2] DOWNING, J. A., and JONES, B. 'Some problems of evaluating i.t.a.—a second experiment'. *Educational Research*, VIII, 100-114.

Conclusions

Therefore, the following generalized conclusions seem to be supported reasonably well by the results of these experiments:

1. i.t.a. as an example of a transitional writing-system for beginning reading and writing in English generally produces superior results in t.o. reading, and in t.o. spelling by the end of the third year of school.

These better results are most marked on tests of word recognition and accuracy in reading t.o., but significant improvements are found also in the speed of reading t.o. In comprehension the result is less clear. The t.o. Neale test showed positive transfer from i.t.a., but the t.o. Standish N.S. 45 Test did not for the group as a whole. There was some evidence, however, from both tests that i.t.a. had helped the slower-learners in respect of comprehension.

The improvements in t.o. reading are most noticeable generally among the highest achievers—those who 'will learn anyway and therefore do not really need educational innovations', according to some British educators. The slower-learning children do begin to show some benefit from i.t.a. at the end of the third year, but the poorest ten per cent. show negligible improvements in test results. It would be fair to say that the research has not been in progress long enough to judge the full effects of i.t.a. on the slower-learning part of the population.

Perhaps surprisingly, t.o. spelling is superior at all levels of achievement among pupils who began with i.t.a., and this seems to be a more generalized transfer effect of the i.t.a. pupils' early experiences of regularity of grapheme-phoneme relations in i.t.a. This may also be the explanation for the superior attainments in arithmetic found in the i.t.a. classes. (The arithmetic data is published elsewhere[1].)

It should be recognized that it is still uncertain how *ultimate* levels of t.o. reading skills and related attainments are affected by beginning with i.t.a., since the research has not yet followed the children into the later stages of education.

2. The success of i.t.a. in improving t.o. literacy skills occurs in spite of an important setback in the growth of these basic skills at the stage of transition from i.t.a. to t.o.

Although subjective impressions of the transition stage suggest that it is a smooth process with no obvious signs of difficulty, the t.o.

---

[1] DOWNING, J. A. (1967). *Evaluating the Initial Teaching Alphabet.* London: Cassell.

test results of the Experimental Group's pupils were generally inferior to their i.t.a. test results obtained a few weeks earlier in the case of the Neale test and a few months earlier in the Schonell test. The exception was the speed of reading which did not show this regression among the higher achieving seventy per cent. of the Experimental Group in the first experiment.

It seems unlikely that this setback is an entirely necessary result of the use of a transitional alphabet for English. The loss of reading ability in changing from i.t.a. to t.o. probably could be reduced by improvements in teaching materials and teachers' methods, especially in regard to the timing of transfer. Generally, in the first experiment, the transition stage tended to begin too early. In the second experiment it appears to have come later, but it seems that the use of i.t.a. requires a longer course than is often contemplated. Certainly for the slow-learners at least it needs to extend into the Junior School.

But of equal importance in considering ways of reducing the setback on transition from i.t.a. to t.o. is the design of the transitional system itself. Evidence from breakdowns of some of the test results confirms the general observations of the Experimenter that i.t.a. is by no means entirely successful in its design for proactive facilitation and contains many sources of proactive interference. It appears that even the superior pupils, who are judged ready for transition by their teachers, may not be transferring in quite the manner originally envisaged. This problem is, of course, related to the question of the timing of the transition stage, but certainly there is a need to consider for the study of this problem a smaller unit of transfer than the upper half of the configurations of whole words.

As has been pointed out, i.t.a. is an *ad hoc* system in which account was not taken of all previous research or even of teachers' experiences. (For example, not until the experiment had begun, was an attempt made to facilitate visual discrimination between *b* and *d*—a problem well known to teachers of beginners and backward readers.) A series of experiments in an experimental psychology laboratory should now be conducted either to shape i.t.a. for this transitional purpose or to produce an entirely new system to maximize the combined effects of simplicity and regularity at the beginning stage and similarity to t.o. on the relevant dimensions for the transition stage. Burt[1] forecast this need at the outset of the experiment: '*Even supposing that these novel proposals turn out, on the whole, to be more*

---

[1] Preface to DOWNING, J. A. (1962). tω bee *or not to be* (later—*The Initial Teaching Alphabet Explained and Illustrated*). London: Cassell.

Conclusions

effective than any of the earlier ones, it still would not follow that they are the best that could be devised'.

It is not possible to compare empirically the results of the i.t.a. experiment with earlier trials of simplified systems, but the subjective evaluations of educators in the i.t.a. experiment do not seem to be any more enthusiastic than those involved in the earlier reforms. Indeed, one is impressed by the similarity of the subjective conclusions drawn by teachers and education officers today and to those voiced on previous occasions.

If the device of a transitional alphabet is to be made fully efficient, then a programme of research on the shaping of the alphabet itself and on the development of teaching techniques and materials clearly should have high priority in the next stage of this line of investigation.

The setback in the growth of literacy skills at the transition stage may be expressed in another way. If the pupils using the simplified and regularized system had been permitted to continue to use it exclusively in their reading and writing, their development of reading and writing skills would almost certainly have continued to improve and would not have been slowed down through the introduction of the more complex and irregular conventional English orthography. This leads to the third, most important, and most definite conclusion that can be drawn from the results of this research.

3. The traditional orthography of English is a serious cause of difficulty in the early stages of learning to read and write.

(*a*) t.o. slowed down children's progress in their series of readers.

(*b*) t.o. caused significantly lower scores on all tests of reading, but especially word recognition and accuracy. The reduction in the learning efficiency of the most able pupils in the t.o. classes was especially remarkable.

(*c*) t.o. also produced markedly inferior results in written composition.

(*d*) t.o. had a seriously limiting effect on the size of the children's written vocabulary.

The unequivocal conclusion from the results of these experiments is that the traditional orthography of English is an important cause of difficulty in teaching and learning reading and writing in English-speaking countries. So long as t.o. is used for beginning reading and writing one must reckon that children are more likely to become confused about the tasks of reading and writing than they would be with a more simple and more regular system for English.

Research Report on the British Experiment with i.t.a.

The question which obviously arises here is the one of spelling reform. If t.o. were displaced entirely by a simplified and more regular system, clearly a saving in the time and efforts of teachers and pupils would result under the current normal everyday conditions as they existed in the schools in these i.t.a. experiments. But spelling reform, though perhaps the simplest and most economical solution from the point of view of the teachers and pupils, is an issue which affects the populations of English-speaking countries in a large number of ways and is therefore not to be decided solely on educational grounds. But, even in education, other solutions may be effective. For example, Carroll[1] suggests that 'Spelling reform . . . might be less necessary if the teaching of reading can be planned so as to circumvent the difficulties of our present system, as seems quite possible.'

Some teachers may feel that no technique of circumventing t.o. would be as immediately effective as changing to a simple and regular system, through a reform of English spelling, and the evidence from this present research, as far as it has gone, lends support to that point of view. A useful contribution to judgment on this issue would be research into the practical problems of introducing such a reform and into its likely outcome. But until such research has been completed and reform admitted as a feasible proposition, there would seem to be an important need to develop further research on ways of circumventing the difficulties of t.o.

Methods of circumventing t.o. may include the use of t.o. itself, but with modified teaching techniques, e.g. the linguistic approach of Bloomfield and Barnhart[2] in which strict regularity of grapheme-phoneme relationship is maintained through absolutely rigorous control of the vocabulary. They may include the use of colour to provide another basis of regularity while preserving the t.o. forms of letters and words, e.g. Gattegno[3] and Jones[4]. And they may include transitional alphabets, such as i.t.a., which, through systematic laboratory studies, could be shaped to provide improved proactive facilitation and reduced proactive interference and thus increase the efficiency of such devices in the transition phase.

[1] CARROLL, J. B. (1953). *The Study of Languages.* Cambridge, Mass.: Harvard University Press.
[2] BLOOMFIELD, L., and BARNHART, C. L. (1961). *Let's Read.* Detroit: Wayne State University Press.
[3] GATTEGNO, C. (1964). 'Words in colour'. *Forward Trends,* 8, 141-144.
[4] JONES, J. K. (1965). 'Colour as an aid to visual perception in early reading'. *British Journal of Educational Psychology,* xxxv, i, 21-27.

Conclusions

If the Initial Teaching Alphabet or some other transitional system is to be taken up and more widely used, as seems likely from current trends, then urgent consideration should be given to this need for a series of laboratory studies to shape the new system to provide greater effectiveness in transfer to reading and writing in the conventional orthography of English.

Tables E1 - 29

Graphs 1 - 36

The Historical Background to the i.t.a. Research Report: a Selected Bibliography

TABLE E1

Progress in Reading Basic Reader Series

Percentage frequency distribution of reading primer reached

Reading Primer Reached	After 1 yr.		After 1⅓ yrs.		After 2 yrs.		After 2⅓ yrs.	
	Exp. (i.t.a.) %	Cont. (t.o.) %	Exp. (i.t.a.) %	Cont. (t.o.) %	Exp. (i.t.a.) %	Cont. (t.o.) %	Exp. (i.t.a.) %	Cont. (t.o.) %
Non-starters	6·6	5·2	2·2	0·3	2·1	0·3	0·7	0
At Books Intro., I or II	55·0	75·9	28·8	54·5	15·6	35·4	9·4	25·9
At Book III	17·8	15·7	12·8	17·2	7·8	17·1	5·0	19·1
At Book IV	10·9	2·8	14·5	13·3	5·1	12·0	4·3	11·2
At Book V	4·0	0·5	8·1	7·2	3·0	4·5	2·5	6·1
Beyond Book V	5·7	0	33·6	7·4	66·4	30·6	78·1	37·8
N	651	651	580	580	333	333	278	278
Median Primer Position	Intro., I, II	Intro., I, II	IV	Intro., I, II	Beyond V	III	Beyond V	IV
Kolmogorov-Smirnov[1] (one-tailed) test χ^2 (2 d. of f.)	49·51		92·71		85·02		90·21	
Per cent. level of significance	0·1		0·1		0·1		0·1	
Superior Group	Exp. (i.t.a.)		Exp. (i.t.a.)		Exp. (i.t.a.)		Exp. (i.t.a.)	

[1] Kolmogorov-Smirnov two-sample test. In SIEGEL, S. (1956). *Nonparametric Statistics for the Behavioral Sciences.* New York and London: McGraw-Hill, pp. 127-136.

Tables

TABLE E2

RESULTS FOR SCHONELL GRADED WORD READING TEST[1] GIVEN AFTER 1 YEAR AND AFTER $1\frac{1}{3}$ YEARS IN i.t.a. TO i.t.a. GROUP AND IN t.o. TO t.o. GROUP.

GROUP	AFTER 1 YEAR				AFTER $1\frac{1}{3}$ YEARS			
	N	MEAN	MEDIAN	Q3-Q1	N	MEAN	MEDIAN	Q3-Q1
Experimental (i.t.a.)	660	17·99	10·15	26·40	585	33·93	30·78	39·04
Control (t.o.)	660	6·61	4·02	7·61	585	14·74	12·23	18·56
Kolmogorov-Smirnov (one-tailed) test χ^2 (2 d. of f.) Per cent. level significance Superior Group	91·79 0·1 Exp. (i.t.a.)				166·91 0·1 Exp. (i.t.a.)			

[1] SCHONELL, F. V., and F. E. (1950). *Graded Word Reading Test*. Edinburgh: Oliver & Boyd.

TABLE E3

READING IN i.t.a. VERSUS READING IN t.o.—ACCURACY

Reading *Accuracy* as measured by the Neale Analysis of Reading Ability Form C. Experimental i.t.a. Group tested in i.t.a., Control t.o. Group tested in t.o.; fifth term.

GROUP	N	MEAN	MEDIAN	Q3-Q1
Experimental	459	24·79	23·44	25·84
Control	459	13·68	9·70	17·99

Significant difference between the two groups at 0·1 per cent. level using Kolmogorov-Smirnov (one-tailed) test. χ^2 (2 d. of f.) = 96·78

TABLE E4

READING IN i.t.a. VERSUS READING IN t.o.—SPEED

Reading *Speed* as measured by the Neale Analysis of Reading Ability Form C. Experimental (i.t.a.) Group tested in i.t.a., Control (t.o.) Group tested in t.o.; fifth term.

GROUP	N	MEAN	MEDIAN	Q3-Q1
Experimental	459	26·41	23·95	21·79
Control	459	24·77	20·62	21·50

Significant difference between the two groups at 5 per cent. level using Kolmogorov-Smirnov (one-tailed) test. χ^2 (2 d. of f.)=7·00

TABLE E5

READING IN i.t.a. VERSUS READING IN t.o.—COMPREHENSION

Reading *Comprehension* as measured by the Neale Analysis of Reading Ability Form C. Experimental (i.t.a.) Group tested in i.t.a., Control (t.o.) Group tested in t.o.; fifth term.

GROUP	N	MEAN	MEDIAN	Q3-Q1
Experimental	459	6·99	6·48	7·28
Control	459	4·86	4·06	5·99

Significant difference between the two groups at 0·1 per cent. level using Kolmogorov-Smirnov (one-tailed) test. χ^2 (2 d. of f.)=46·18

Tables

TABLE E6

TRANSFER OF LEARNING FROM i.t.a. TO t.o.—ACCURACY

(All experimental sub-sample pupils tested)

Reading *Accuracy* as measured by the Neale Analysis of Reading Ability[1] in Experimental (i.t.a.) Group only. i.t.a. test and t.o. test results of *same subjects*; fifth term.

TEST	N	MEAN	MEDIAN	Q3-Q1
i.t.a. (Form C) ..	433	25·36	24·02	26·16
t.o. (Form A) ..	433	18·88	18·28	24·96

i.t.a. scores superior. Significant difference between the two groups at 0·1 per cent. level using Wilcoxon[2] matched-pairs signed-ranks test (two-tailed): $Z=16·76$

TABLE E7

TRANSFER OF LEARNING FROM i.t.a. TO t.o.—SPEED

(All experimental sub-sample pupils tested)

Reading *Speed* as measured by Neale Analysis of Reading Ability in Experimental (i.t.a.) Group only. i.t.a. test and t.o. test results of *same subjects*; fifth term.

TEST	N	MEAN	MEDIAN	Q3-Q1
i.t.a. (Form C) ..	433	27·04	24·32	21·85
t.o. (Form A) ..	433	32·00	27·99	36·27

t.o. speed superior. Significant difference between the two groups at 0·1 per cent. level using Wilcoxon matched-pairs signed-ranks test (two-tailed): $Z=5·71$

[1] NEALE, M. D. (1958). *Neale Analysis of Reading Ability* (three parallel forms: A, B and C). London: Macmillan.
[2] Wilcoxon matched-pairs signed-ranks test. In SIEGEL, S. (1956). *Nonparametric Statistics for the Behavioral Sciences*. New York and London: McGraw-Hill., pp. 75-83.

Research Report on the British Experiment with i.t.a.

TABLE E8

TRANSFER OF LEARNING FROM i.t.a. TO t.o.—COMPREHENSION

(All experimental sub-sample pupils tested)

Reading *Comprehension* as measured by Neale Analysis of Reading Ability in Experimental (i.t.a.) Group only. i.t.a. test and t.o. test results of *same subjects*; fifth term.

TEST	N	MEAN	MEDIAN	Q3-Q1
i.t.a. (Form C)	433	6·92	6·68	7·30
t.o. (Form A)	433	6·15	6·06	7·77

i.t.a. scores superior. Significant difference between the two groups at 0·1 per cent. level using Wilcoxon matched-pairs signed-ranks test (two-tailed): $Z = 4·037$

TABLE E9

TRANSFER OF LEARNING FROM i.t.a. TO t.o. IN EXPERIMENTAL GROUP PUPILS—ACCURACY

Pupils transferred to t.o. reading by teachers

Reading *Accuracy* as measured by Neale Analysis of Reading Ability. Only Experimental (i.t.a.) Group subjects 'transferred' to t.o. books by teachers at least 6 weeks prior to administration of t.o. Neale Test Form A.

TEST	N	MEAN	MEDIAN	Q3-Q1
i.t.a. (Form C)	152	42·2	38·03	22·24
t.o. (Form A)	152	33·4	30·31	16·13

Earlier Neale C i.t.a. scores significantly superior to later Neale A t.o. scores at 0·1 per cent. level of confidence using Wilcoxon matched-pairs signed-ranks test (two-tailed): $Z = 7·14$

Tables

TABLE E10

TRANSFER OF LEARNING FROM i.t.a. TO t.o. IN EXPERIMENTAL GROUP PUPILS—SPEED

Pupils transferred to t.o. reading by teachers

Reading *Speed* as measured by Neale Analysis of Reading Ability. Only Experimental (i.t.a.) Group subjects 'transferred' to t.o. books by teachers at least 6 weeks prior to administration of t.o. Neale Test Form A.

TEST	N	MEAN SPEED (*words per min.*)	MEDIAN	Q3-Q1
i.t.a. (Form C) ..	152	40·6	35·00	23·95
t.o. (Form A) ..	152	53·5	53·06	29·33

Later Neale A t.o. speed significantly faster than earlier Neale C i.t.a. speed at 0·1 per cent. level of confidence using Wilcoxon matched-pairs signed-ranks test (two-tailed): $Z=6·93$

TABLE E11

TRANSFER OF LEARNING FROM i.t.a. TO t.o. IN EXPERIMENTAL GROUP PUPILS—COMPREHENSION

Pupils transferred to t.o. reading by teachers

Reading *Comprehension* as measured by Neale Analysis of Reading Ability. Only Experimental (i.t.a.) Group subjects 'transferred' to t.o. books by teachers at least 6 weeks prior to administration of Neale Test Form A.

TEST	N	MEAN	MEDIAN	Q3-Q1
i.t.a. (Form C) ..	152	10·8	10·04	7·04
t.o. (Form A) ..	152	9·9	9·47	6·46

Earlier Neale C i.t.a. comprehension score significantly superior to later Neale A t.o. score at 1 per cent. level of confidence using Wilcoxon matched-pairs signed-ranks test (two-tailed): $Z=3·04$

Research Report on the British Experiment with i.t.a.

TABLE E12

Transfer of Learning from i.t.a. to t.o.—Word Recognition

(All experimental group pupils tested)

Schonell Graded Word Reading Test given in i.t.a. in fifth term (after 1⅓ years) and in t.o. in seventh term (third year). i.t.a. and t.o. test results of *same subjects*.

Test	N	Mean	Median	Q3-Q1
Schonell i.t.a. ..	257	36·49	31·38	44·42
Schonell t.o. ..	257	31·54	29·02	29·76

Earlier i.t.a. scores superior. Significant difference at 0·1 per cent. level, using Wilcoxon matched-pairs signed-ranks test (two-tailed): Z=4·06

TABLE E13

Transfer of Learning from i.t.a. to t.o. in Experimental Group—Word Recognition

Only pupils transferred to t.o. reading by teachers

Schonell Graded Word Reading Test scores for only those Experimental Group subjects who were transferred to t.o. books at least four months prior to Schonell Test in t.o. at start of second school year.

Test	N	Mean	Median	Q3-Q1
Schonell i.t.a. ..	135	51·63	49·64	41·65
Schonell t.o. ..	135	44·82	39·63	32·46

Earlier i.t.a. scores superior. Significant difference at 0·1 per cent. level using Wilcoxon matched-pairs signed-ranks test (two-tailed): Z=3·79

Tables

TABLE E14

ANALYSIS OF ERRORS MADE IN THE t.o. EDITION OF SCHONELL'S GRADED WORD READING TEST BY 135 EXPERIMENTAL GROUP SUBJECTS TRANSFERRED TO t.o. READING BY THEIR TEACHERS

(First fifty words set out in graded order of difficulty according to Schonell.)

Schonell's Order	Word t.o.	Word i.t.a.	Number of Errors	Schonell's Order	Word t.o.	Word i.t.a.	Number of Errors
1	tree	tree	1	26	crowd	croud	18
2	little	liitl	0	27	sandwich	sandwich	15
3	milk	milk	0	28	beginning	beginning	31
4	egg	egg	0	29	postage	postæj	47
5	book	book	3	30	island	ieland	67
6	school	scωl	7	31	saucer	sauser	46
7	sit	sit	1	32	angel	anjel	33
8	frog	frog	1	33	ceiling	seeling	79
9	playing	plaeiŋ	6	34	appeared	appeerd	47
10	bun	bun	3	35	gnome	nœm	68
11	flower	flouer	6	36	canary	canary	90
12	road	rœd	12	37	attractive	attractiv	67
13	clock	clock	3	38	imagine	imajin	62
14	train	træn	4	39	nephew	nevue	71
15	light	liet	13	40	gradually	gradueally	63
16	picture	pictuer	12	41	smoulder	smœlder	58
17	think	think	5	42	applaud	applaud	72
18	summer	summer	2	43	disposal	dispœsal	68
19	people	peepl	14	44	nourished	nurisht	74
20	something	sumthiŋ	4	45	diseased	diseesd	77
21	dream	dreem	22	46	university	ueniversity	68
22	downstairs	dounstærs	18	47	orchestra	orcestra	95
23	biscuit	biscit	19	48	knowledge	nœledʒ	95
24	shepherd	ʃheperd	13	49	audience	audiens	79
25	thirsty	thirsty	21	50	situated	situæated	81

TABLE E15

ANALYSIS OF ERRORS MADE IN THE t.o. EDITION OF NEALE TEST BY 152 EXPERIMENTAL GROUP SUBJECTS TRANSFERRED TO t.o. READING BY THEIR TEACHERS
(First 3 passages of Neale Test Form A.)

Words		Number of Errors	Words		Number of Errors
t.o.	i.t.a.		t.o.	i.t.a.	
A	a	1	a	a	1
black	black	1	pet	pet	2
cat	cat	1	Tom	tom	6
came	cæm	7	stopped	stoppt	16
to	to	1	on	on	1
my	mie	2	his way	his wæ	4
house	hous	2	to school	to scool	2
She	ſhee	5	The milkman's	the milkman's	5
put	pot	0	horse had	hors had	11
her	her	6	wandered	wonderd	37
kitten	kitten	3	in the fog	in the fog	6
by	bie	2	The horse	ſhe hors	8
the	the	1	and cart	and cart	16
door	dor	2	blocked	blockt	26
Then	ſhen	5	the centre	ſhe senter	82
she	ſhee	1	of the road	ov the rœd	7
went	went	0	Traffic	traffic	12
away	awæ	1	was coming	wɔs cuming	8
Now	nou	15	There was	ſhær wɔs	6
I	ie	2	no	nœ	11
have	hav	1	time	tiem	4
her	her	1	to call	to caull	7
baby	bæby	3	the milkman	ſhe milkman	1
for	for	1	Quickly	kwickly	27

Tables

TABLE E15—*continued*

Words		Number of Errors	Words		Number of Errors
t.o.	i.t.a.		t.o.	i.t.a.	
Tom	tom	4	stumbled	stumbld	37
led	led	3	Her whip fell	her whip fell	26
the horse	ƒhe hors	5	The youngest	ƒhe yungest	25
to safety	too sæfty	41	lion sprang	lieon spraŋ	29
just as the	just az ƒhe	2	towards her	towaurds her	28
frightened	frietend	51	Swiftly	swiftly	18
milkman	milkman	2	Jack leaped	jack lept	52
returned	returnd	39	inside the cage	insied ƒhe cæj	34
The lions'	ƒhe lieons'	12	cracking the	crackiŋ ƒhe	33
final	fienal	72	whip with	whip with	16
act was	act woz	23	great skill	græt skill	38
in progress	in progress	66	His prompt	his prompt	65
Jack stood	jack stood	7	action	acƒhon	72
waiting to	wætiŋ too	21	enabled	enæbld	87
clear the ring	cleer the riŋ	26	Tess to regain	tess too regan	85
Tonight the	tooniet ƒhe	52	control quickly	controel kwickly	49
thunder	thunder	21	During	dueriŋ	57
outside the	outsied ƒhe	23	that brief	that breef	54
circus tent	sircus tent	28	adventure	adventuer	35
had made the	had mæd ƒhe	18	however Jack	houever jack	27
lions restless	lieons restless	44	had decided	had desieded	67
Suddenly Tess	suddenly tess	25	upon his	upon his	17
the lion trainer	ƒhe lieon træner	59	future work	fuetuer wurk	81

TABLE E16

TRANSFER OF LEARNING FROM i.t.a. to t.o.—ACCURACY

All 171 Experimental Group subjects who were tested on all three occasions of the administration of the Neale Analysis of Reading Ability.

TEST	TIME	N	MEAN	MEDIAN	Q3-Q1
i.t.a. (Form C)	Fifth term	171	28·79	25·64	27·74
t.o. (Form A)	Fifth term	171	21·31	20·00	25·10
t.o. (Form B)	End of 3rd year	171	39·98	39·83	27·33

TABLE E17

TRANSFER OF LEARNING FROM i.t.a. TO t.o.—SPEED

All 171 Experimental Group subjects who were tested on all three occasions of the administration of the Neale Analysis of Reading Ability.

TEST	TIME	N	MEAN	MEDIAN	Q3-Q1
i.t.a. (Form C)	Fifth term	171	29·47	26·93	23·08
t.o. (Form A)	Fifth term	171	36·80	34·96	36·06
t.o. (Form B)	End of 3rd year	171	60·73	61·65	39·93

TABLE E18

TRANSFER OF LEARNING FROM i.t.a. to t.o.—COMPREHENSION

All 171 Experimental Group subjects who were tested on all three occasions of the administration of the Neale Analysis of Reading Ability.

TEST	TIME	N	MEAN	MEDIAN	Q3-Q1
i.t.a. (Form C)	Fifth term	171	8·18	7·86	8·56
t.o. (Form A)	Fifth term	171	7·16	6·95	8·44
t.o. (Form B)	End of 3rd year	171	15·36	13·52	11·91

Tables

TABLE E19

READING IN t.o. AT MID-SECOND YEAR—ACCURACY

Reading *Accuracy* as measured by Neale Analysis of Reading Ability Form A. Experimental and Control Groups both tested *in t.o.*

Group	N	Mean	Median	Q3-Q1
Experimental	457	18·61	16·93	25·40
Control	457	16·90	14·76	22·98

Difference between the two groups not significant at 5 per cent. level, using Kolmogorov-Smirnov (one-tailed) test. χ^2 (2 d. of f.) $=4·48$

TABLE E20

READING IN t.o. AT MID-SECOND YEAR—SPEED

Reading *Speed* as measured by Neale Analysis of Reading Ability Form A. Experimental and Control Groups both tested *in t.o.*

Group	N	Mean	Median	Q3-Q1
Experimental	457	31·33	27·36	36·58
Control	457	29·99	27·28	30·72

Difference between the two groups not significant at 5 per cent. level, using Kolmogorov-Simirnov (one-tailed) test. χ^2 (2 d. of f.)$=2·33$

TABLE E21

READING IN t.o. AT MID-SECOND YEAR—COMPREHENSION

Reading *Comprehension* as measured by Neale Analysis of Reading Ability Form A. Experimental and Control Groups both tested *in t.o.*

Group	N	Mean	Median	Q3-Q1
Experimental	457	6·24	5·88	7·88
Control	457	5·87	5·22	7·31

Difference between the two groups not significant at 5 per cent. level, using Kolmogorov-Smirnov (one-tailed) test. χ^2 (2 d. of f.) $=2·52$

Research Report on the British Experiment with i.t.a.

TABLE E22

Word Recognition in t.o. at beginning of third year
(middle of seventh term)

Results for Schonell Graded Word Reading Test given in t.o. to both Experimental and Control Groups.

Group	N	Mean	Median	Q3-Q1
Experimental	291	29·70	26·94	28·10
Control	291	24·39	23·31	24·32

Experimental i.t.a. Group superior. Significant difference between the two groups at 5 per cent. level using Kolmogorov-Smirnov (one-tailed) test. χ^2 (2 d. of f.)=6·59

TABLE E23

Reading in t.o. at end of three school years—Accuracy

Reading *Accuracy* as measured by Neale Analysis of Reading Ability Form B. Experimental and Control Groups both tested *in t.o.*

Group	N	Mean	Median	Q3-Q1
Experimental	194	38·97	38·28	27·71
Control	194	31·66	30·23	27·89

Experimental i.t.a. Group superior. Significant difference between the two groups at the 1 per cent. level using Kolmogorov-Smirnov (one-tailed) test. χ^2 (2 d. of f.)=10·55

TABLE E24

Reading in t.o. at end of three school years—Speed

Reading *Speed* as measured by Neale Analysis of Reading Ability Form B. Experimental and Control Groups both tested *in t.o.*

Group	N	Mean	Median	Q3-Q1
Experimental	194	59·07	61·00	41·55
Control	194	51·59	49·39	43·57

Experimental i.t.a. Group superior. Significant difference between the two groups at 1 per cent. level using Kolmogorov-Smirnov (one-tailed) test. χ^2 (2 d. of f.)=9·29

Tables

TABLE E25

READING IN t.o. AT END OF THREE SCHOOL YEARS
—COMPREHENSION

Reading *Comprehension* as measured by Neale Analysis of Reading Ability Form B. Experimental and Control Groups both tested *in t.o.*

Group	N	Mean	Median	Q3-Q1
Experimental ..	194	14·77	14·24	12·01
Control	194	12·60	11·24	12·33

Experimental i.t.a. group superior. Significant difference between the two groups at 1 per cent. level, using Kolmogorov-Smirnov (one-tailed) test. χ^2 (2 d. of f.) = 9·92

TABLE E26

SILENT READING COMPREHENSION IN t.o. AT END OF SECOND AND THIRD SCHOOL YEARS

Standish N.S. 45 Test

Group	Two-year-taught				Three-year-taught			
	N	Mean	Median	Q3-Q1	N	Mean	Median	Q3-Q1
Experimental (i.t.a.) ..	160	9·69	6·63	13·32	175	15·70	17·12	14·48
Control (t.o.)	160	11·81	10·40	16·46	175	15·03	16·12	18·17
Kolmogorov-Smirnov (one-tailed) test χ^2 (2d. of f.) Per cent. level of significance	5·00 N.S.				2·57 N.S.			

Research Report on the British Experiment with i.t.a.

TABLE E27

STAFFORDSHIRE STUDY OF WRITTEN COMPOSITION
RESULTS OF WORD ANALYSIS

t.o. SCHOOLS				i.t.a. SCHOOLS			
SCHOOL 1	\multicolumn{3}{c}{VOCABULARY}	**SCHOOL 6**	\multicolumn{3}{c}{VOCABULARY}			
Type of Word	*Net*	*Repetitions*	*Total*	*Type of Word*	*Net*	*Repetitions*	*Total*
'Basic'	57·9	98·9	156·8	'Basic' ..	67·4	139·3	206·7
More advanced	32·3	7·8	40·1	More advanced	29·9	10·3	40·2
TOTAL	90·2	106·7	196·9	TOTAL ..	97·3	149·6	256·9
SCHOOL 2	\multicolumn{3}{c}{VOCABULARY}				
Type of Word	*Net*	*Repetitions*	*Total*				
'Basic' ..	39·6	51·3	90·9	**SCHOOL 7**	\multicolumn{3}{c}{VOCABULARY}
More advanced	17·1	5·1	22·2	*Type of Word*	*Net*	*Repetitions*	*Total*
TOTAL ..	56·7	56·4	113·1	'Basic' ..	53·1	118·3	171·4
				More advanced	30·2	11·6	41·8
SCHOOL 3	\multicolumn{3}{c}{VOCABULARY}	TOTAL ..	83·3	129·9	213·2
Type of Word	*Net*	*Repetitions*	*Total*				
'Basic' ..	25·4	26·1	51·5				
More advanced	8·3	2·4	10·7				
				SCHOOL 8	\multicolumn{3}{c}{VOCABULARY}
TOTAL ..	33·7	28·5	62·2	*Type of Word*	*Net*	*Repetitions*	*Total*
SCHOOL 4	\multicolumn{3}{c}{VOCABULARY}	'Basic' ..	63·6	151·1	214·7
Type of Word	*Net*	*Repetitions*	*Total*	More advanced	33·3	14·2	47·5
'Basic' ..	57·1	102·9	160·0	TOTAL ..	96·9	165·3	262·2
More advanced	24·9	11·1	36·0				
TOTAL ..	82·0	114·0	196·0				
SCHOOL 5	\multicolumn{3}{c}{VOCABULARY}	**SCHOOL 9**	\multicolumn{3}{c}{VOCABULARY}
Type of Word	*Net*	*Repetitions*	*Total*	*Type of Word*	*Net*	*Repetitions*	*Total*
'Basic' ..	28·7	36·7	65·4	'Basic' ..	58·9	113·3	172·2
More advanced	8·3	3·7	12·0	More advanced	28·1	6·4	34·5
TOTAL ..	37·0	40·4	77·4	TOTAL ..	87·0	119·7	206·7

TABLE E28

t.o. spelling in Experimental (i.t.a.) and Control (t.o.) Groups as Measured by Schonell Graded Word Spelling Test

Group	Form A Mid-third Year				Form B Mid-fourth Year			
	N	Mean	Median	Q3-Q1	N	Mean	Median	Q3-Q1
Experimental..	374	28·44	25·96	19·45	102	39·11	39·44	27·29
Control ..	374	25·34	24·69	19·72	102	32·25	32·08	21·78
Kolmogorov-Smirnov (one-tailed) test χ^2 (2d. of f.) Per cent. level of significance Superior group	4·49 N.S. —				6·35 5 Exp. (i.t.a.)			

TABLE E29

EFFECTIVENESS OF MANIPULATION OF HAWTHORNE EFFECT IN CONTROL GROUP
Standish N.S. 45 Test

Year	School Number	Pre-research Pupils		Pupils in Research Project		Kolmogorov-Smirnov (one-tailed) Test	Superior Group (Where $P<\cdot05$)
		N	Mean Score	N	Mean Score		
1961	1	29	17·31	31	20·90	N.S. $\chi^2 =$ 4·94	
	2	32	19·09	17	21·24	N.S. $\chi^2 =$ 1·59	
	3	53	16·21	60	11·48	** $\chi^2 =$ 12·03	Pre-research
	4	66	15·65	37	18·95	N.S. $\chi^2 =$ 3·95	
	5	31	10·32	25	5·20	** $\chi^2 =$ 12·62	Pre-research
	6	24	24·67	31	21·71	N.S. $\chi^2 =$ 1·66	
	7	66	9·79	26	9·88	N.S. $\chi^2 =$ 1·32	
	8	72	10·76	74	11·27	N.S. $\chi^2 =$ 1·38	
	9	31	11·45	19	12·11	N.S. $\chi^2 =$ 0·43	
	10	52	11·69	35	9·34	N.S. $\chi^2 =$ 5·47	
	11	21	21·57	10	22·00	N.S. $\chi^2 =$ 0·35	
	12	36	18·00	35	18·00	N.S. $\chi^2 =$ 0·26	
	13	148	12·30	47	7·83	** $\chi^2 =$ 16·96	Pre-research
	14	55	14·45	39	18·05	* $\chi^2 =$ 6·86	Research
1962	15	26	15·11	25	14·80	N.S. $\chi^2 =$ 0·04	
	16	56	8·52	35	10·83	N.S. $\chi^2 =$ 2·13	
	17	46	20·06	33	18·97	N.S. $\chi^2 =$ 1·30	
	18	44	17·36	31	16·06	N.S. $\chi^2 =$ 0·56	
	19	34	9·38	25	13·00	* $\chi^2 =$ 6·03	Research
	20	98	16·03	53	13·87	N.S. $\chi^2 =$ 1·28	
	21	76	13·55	61	11·56	N.S. $\chi^2 =$ 1·26	
	22	45	15·89	42	12·57	N.S. $\chi^2 =$ 3·15	
	23	18	24·94	58	26·28	* $\chi^2 =$ 6·63	Research
	24	167	14·06	27	12·44	N.S. $\chi^2 =$ 0·96	
	25	86	11·24	33	14·52	N.S. $\chi^2 =$ 2·62	
	26	61	10·21	21	9·52	N.S. $\chi^2 =$ 2·82	
	27	126	10·31	17	1·88	*** $\chi^2 =$ 15·75	Pre-research
	28	41	6·98	26	11·42	N.S. $\chi^2 =$ 4·42	
1963	29	35	12·26	30	13·17	N.S. $\chi^2 =$ 0·65	
	30	39	14·15	21	17·29	N.S. $\chi^2 =$ 1·30	
		1,714		1,024			

Significant levels for χ^2 (2 d. of f.) *5 per cent. $\chi^2=5\cdot99$ **1 per cent. $\chi^2=9\cdot21$ ***0·1 per cent. $\chi^2=13\cdot82$

COMPARATIVE PROGRESS THROUGH BASIC READER SERIES OVER TEN RANGES OF ACHIEVEMENT

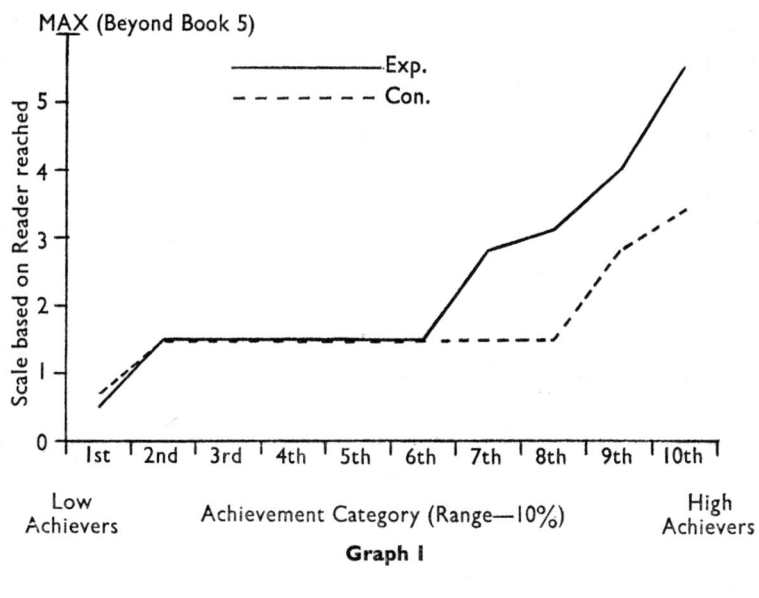

Graph 1

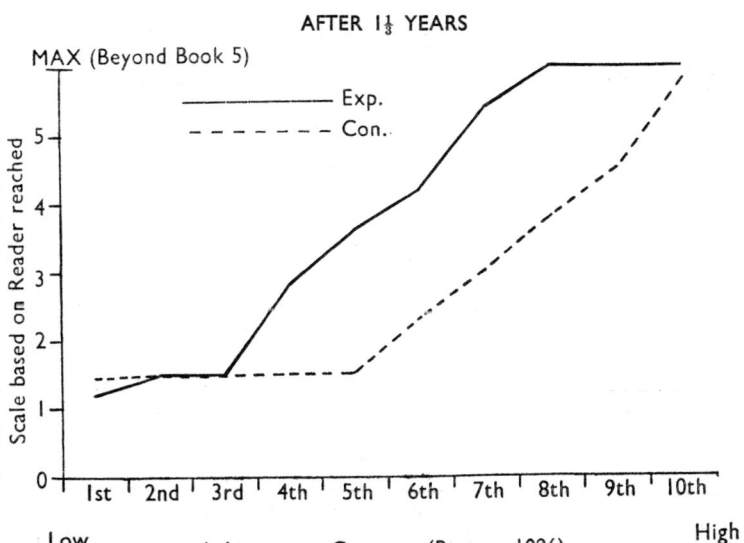

Graph 2

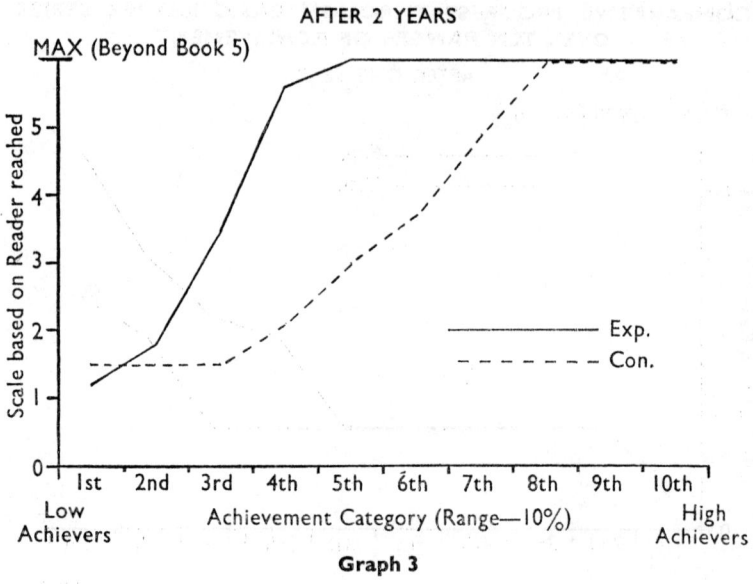

Graph 3

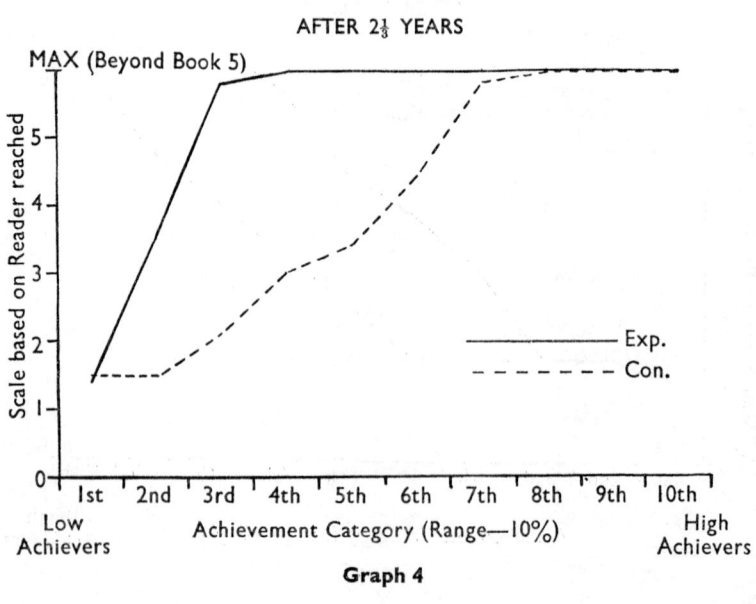

Graph 4

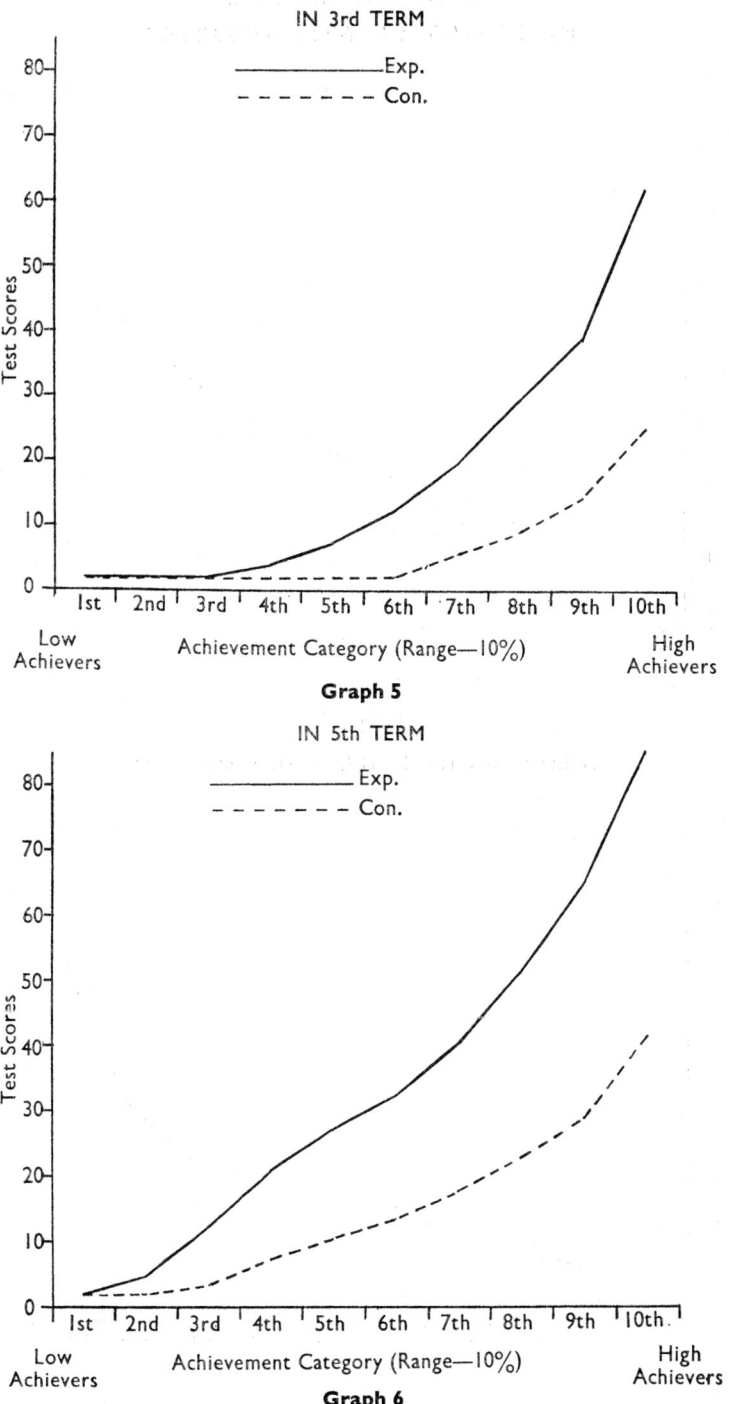

SCORES ON SCHONELL GRADED WORD READING TEST OVER TEN RANGES OF ACHIEVEMENT

Graph 5

Graph 6

SCORES ON NEALE ANALYSIS OF READING ABILITY OVER TEN RANGES OF ACHIEVEMENT

FORM C — AFTER 1½ YEARS — ACCURACY

Graph 7

FORM C — AFTER 1½ YEARS — READING RATE

Graph 8

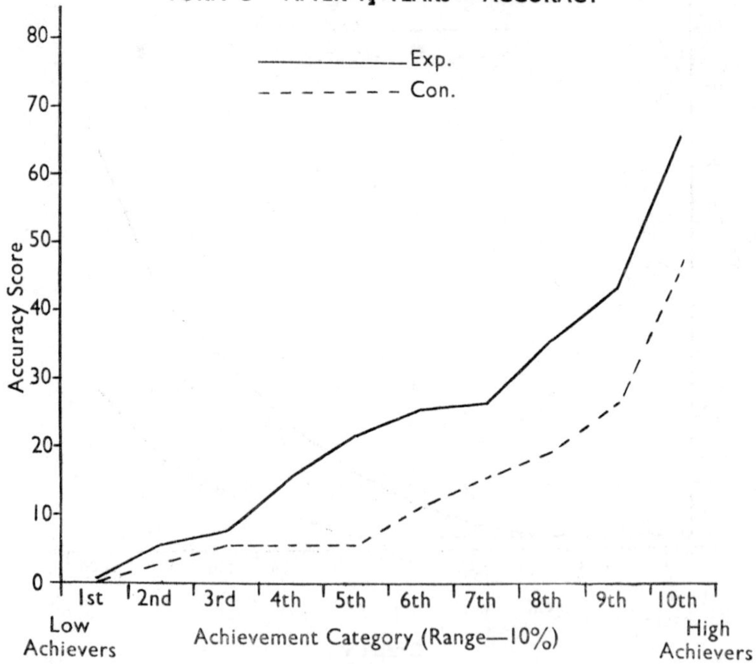

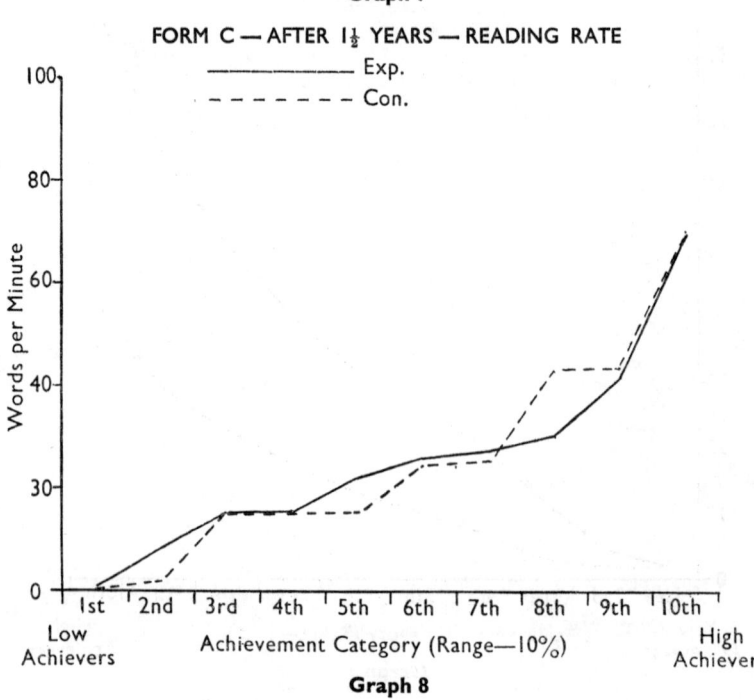

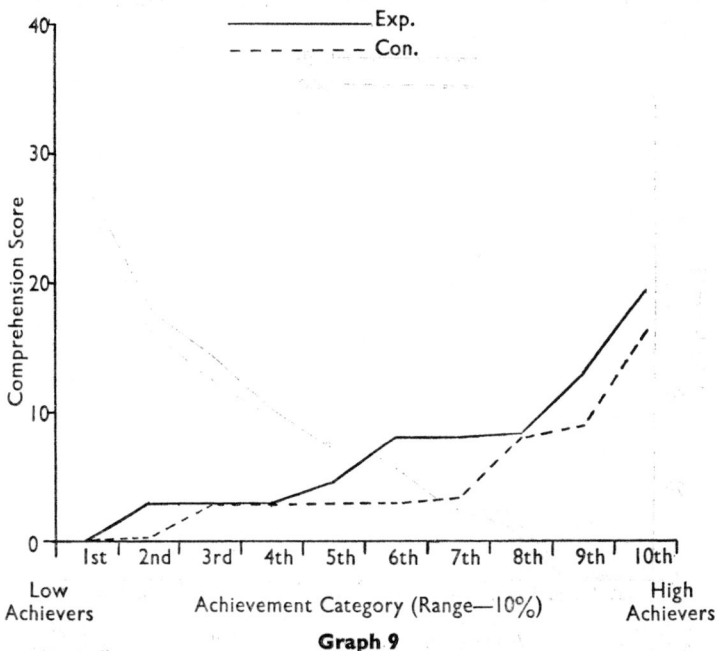

Graph 9

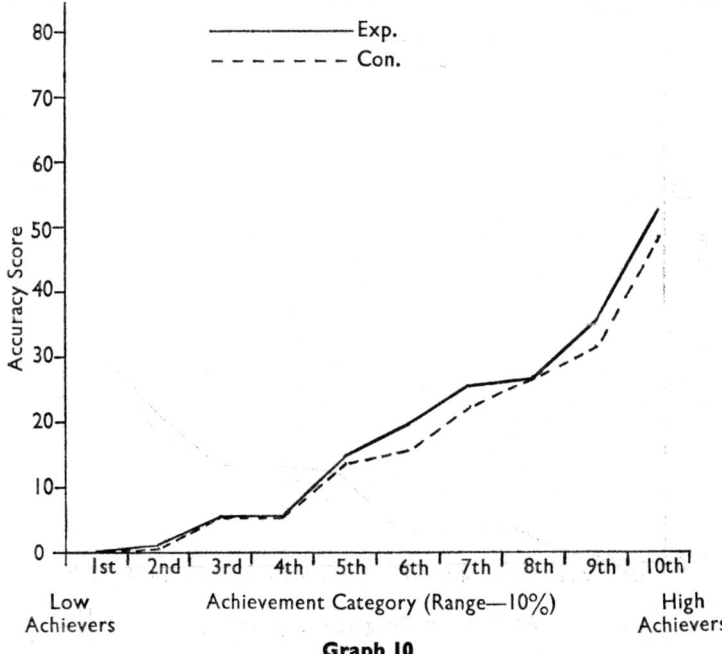

Graph 10

FORM A (in t.o. to both groups) — AFTER 1½ YEARS — READING RATE

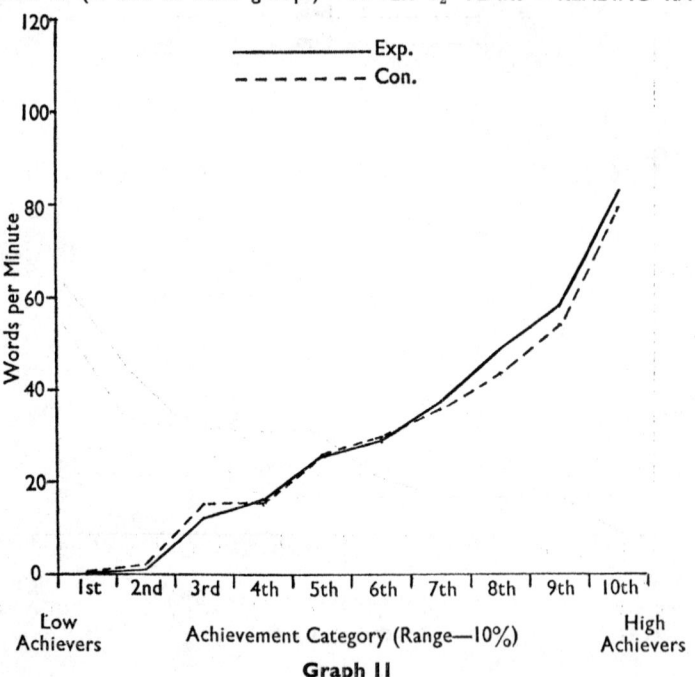

Graph 11

FORM A (in t.o. to both groups) — AFTER 1½ YEARS — COMPREHENSION

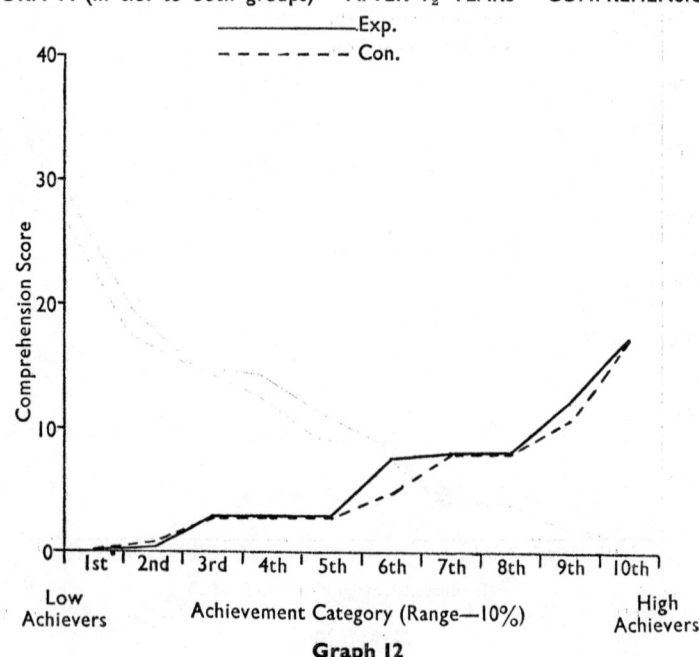

Graph 12

Experimental Group's Accuracy scores in i.t.a. and in t.o. over ten ranges of achievement

NEALE FORM C (i.t.a.) AND FORM A (t.o.) — AFTER 1½ YEARS

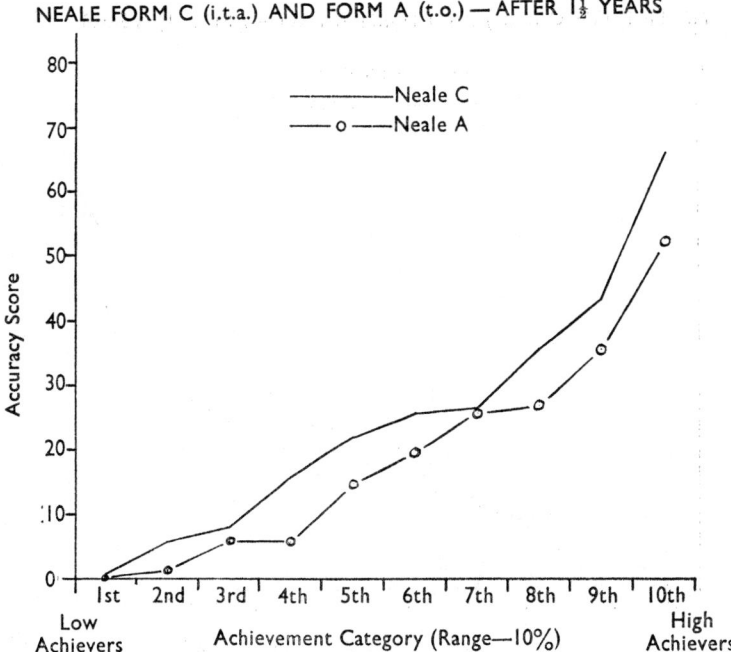

Graph 13

Control Group's Accuracy scores in t.o. over ten ranges of achievement: test and retest

NEALE FORMS C AND A (both in t.o.) — AFTER 1½ YEARS

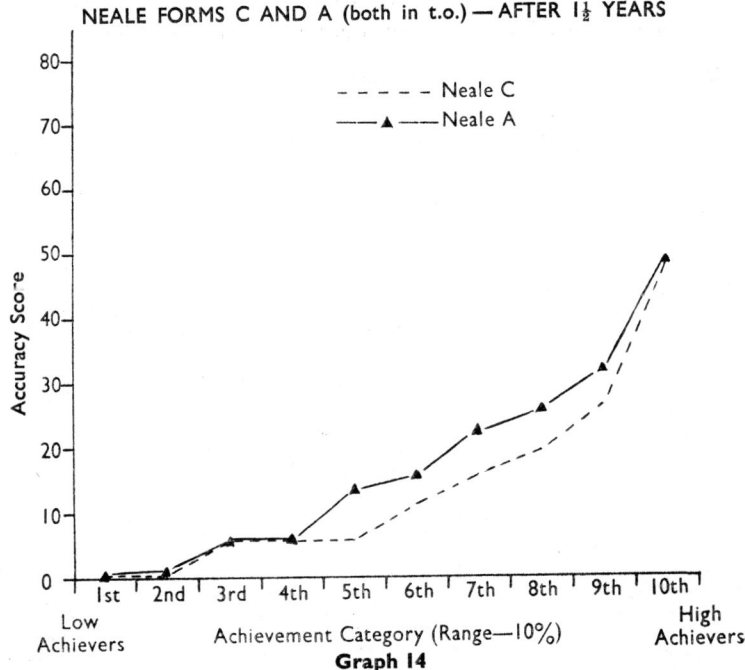

Graph 14

Experimental Group's Reading Rate scores in i.t.a. and t.o. over ten ranges of achievement

NEALE FORM C (i.t.a.) AND FORM A (t.o.) — AFTER 1½ YEARS

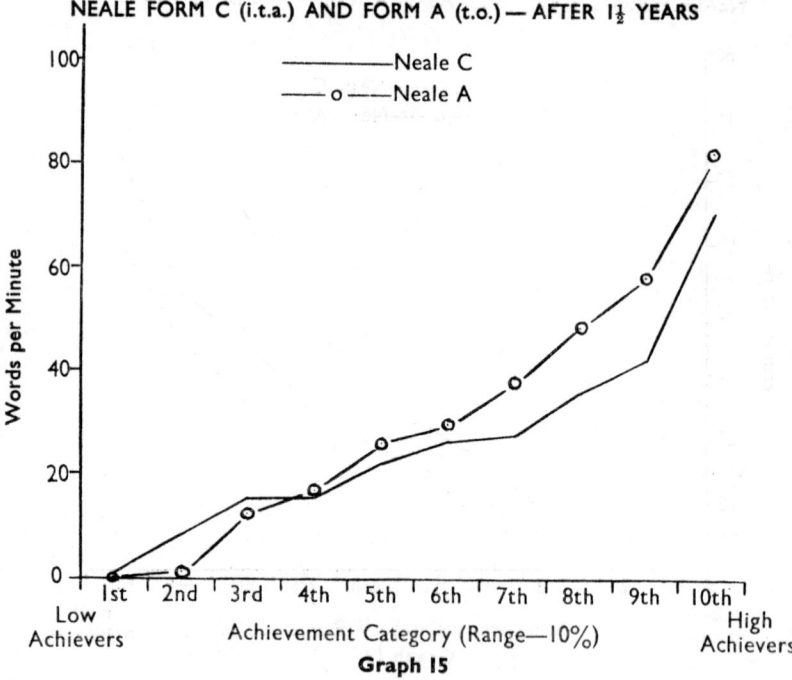

Graph 15

Control Group's Reading Rate scores in t.o. over ten ranges of achievement: test and retest

NEALE FORMS C AND A (both in t.o.) — AFTER 1½ YEARS

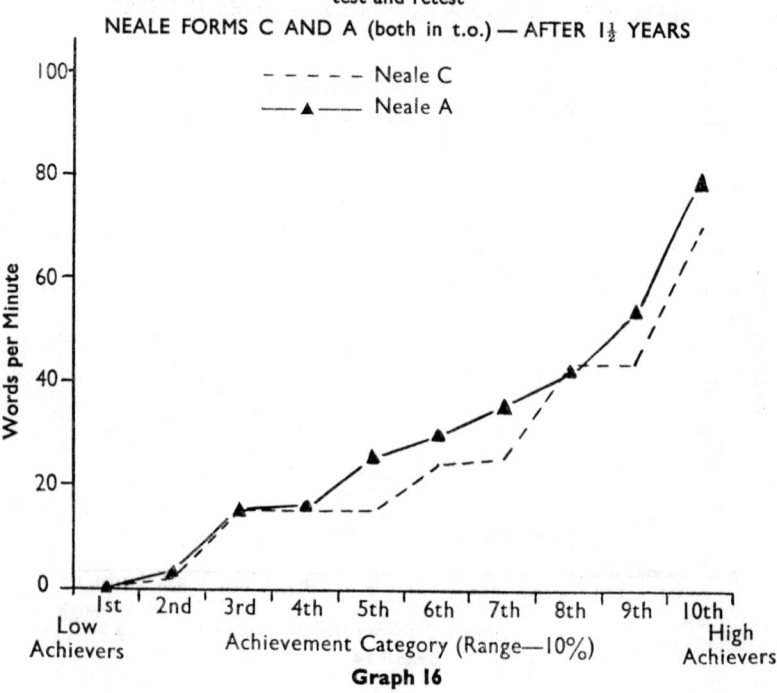

Graph 16

Experimental Group's Comprehension scores in i.t.a. and t.o. over ten ranges of achievement
NEALE FORM C (i.t.a.) AND FORM A (t.o.) — AFTER 1½ YEARS

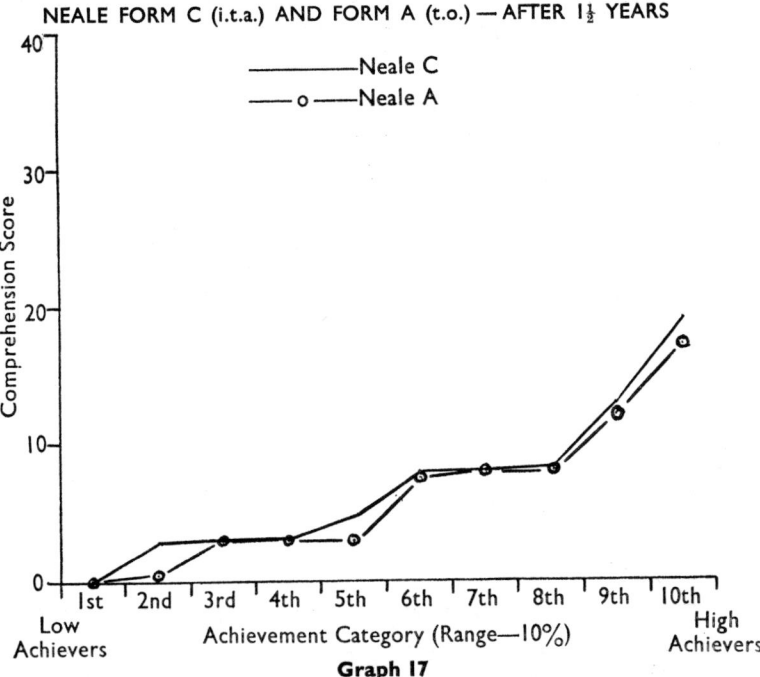

Graph 17

Control Group's Comprehension scores in t.o. over ten ranges of achievement: test and retest
NEALE FORMS C AND A (both in t.o.) — AFTER 1½ YEARS

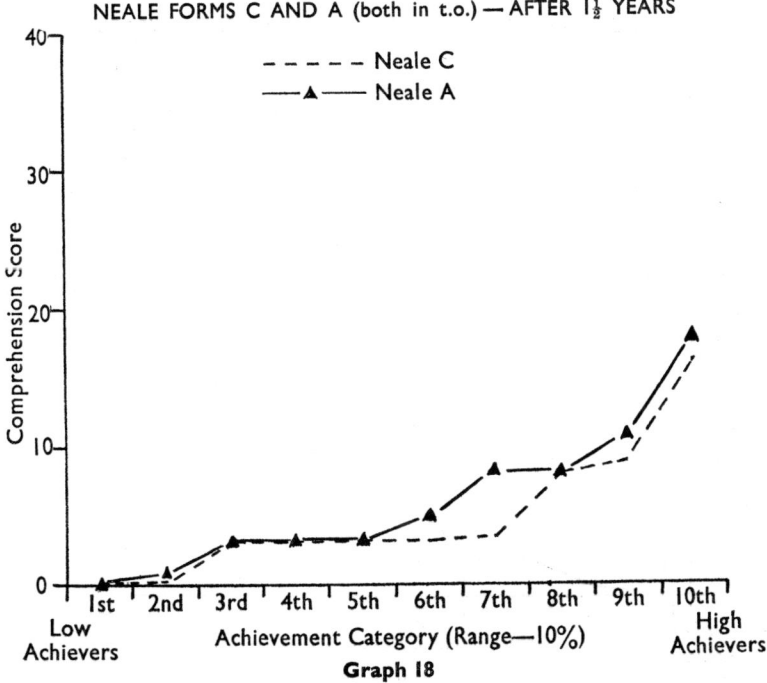

Graph 18

Neale Analysis (Form B) in t.o. to both groups over ten ranges of achievement
AFTER 3 YEARS — ACCURACY

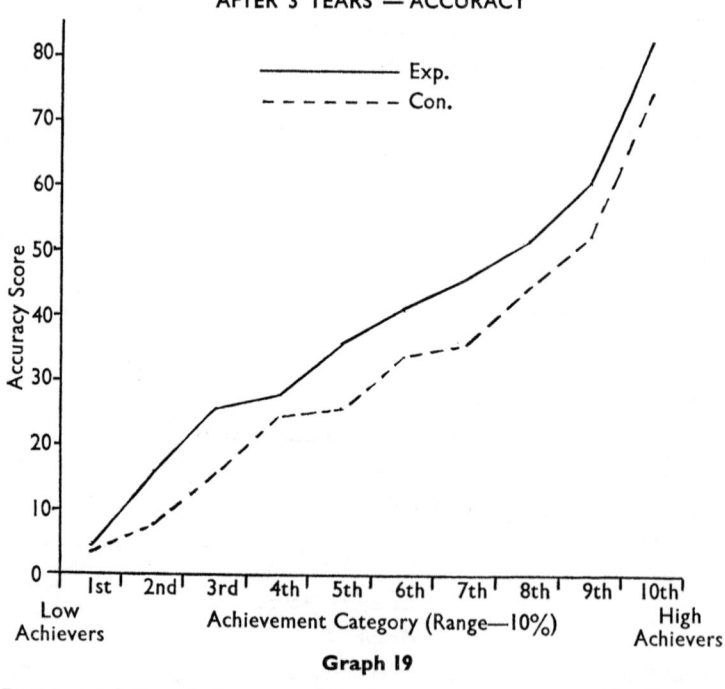

Graph 19

Experimental Group's Accuracy scores in t.o. over ten ranges of achievement
NEALE A — AFTER 1½ YEARS, NEALE B — AFTER 3 YEARS

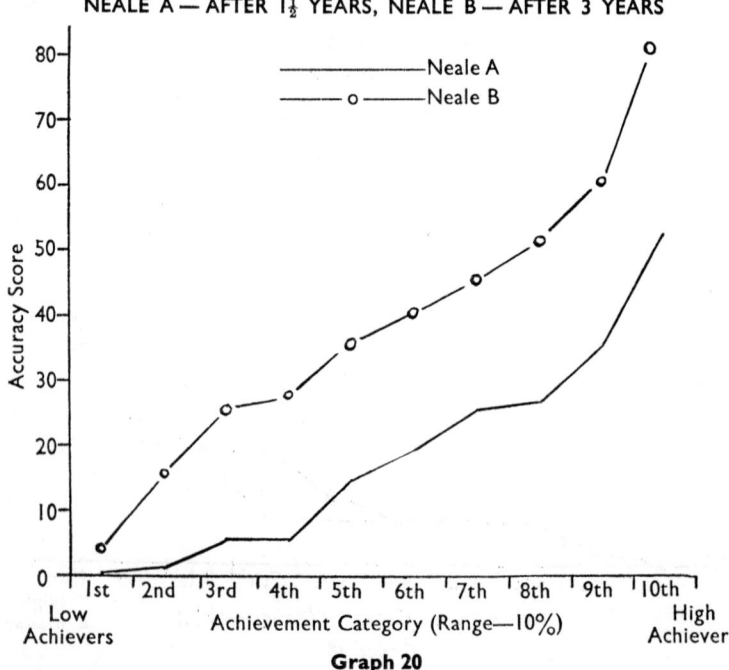

Graph 20

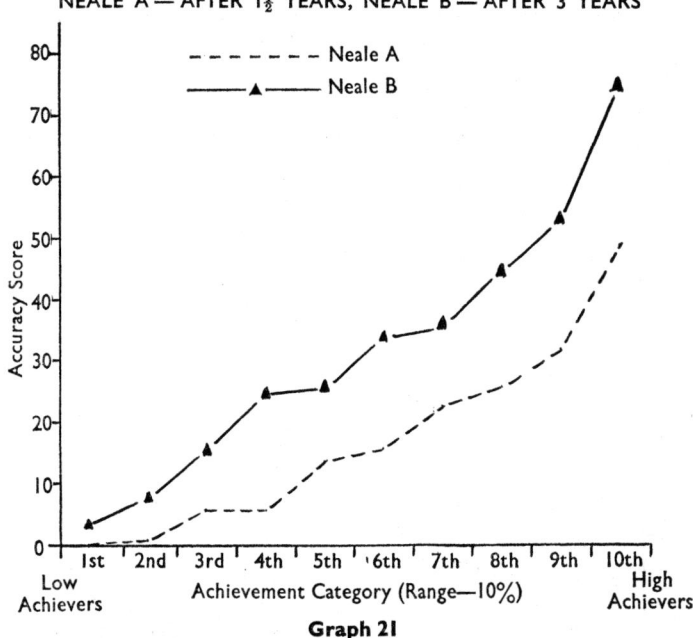

Control Group's Accuracy scores in t.o. over ten ranges of achievement
NEALE A — AFTER 1½ YEARS, NEALE B — AFTER 3 YEARS

Graph 21

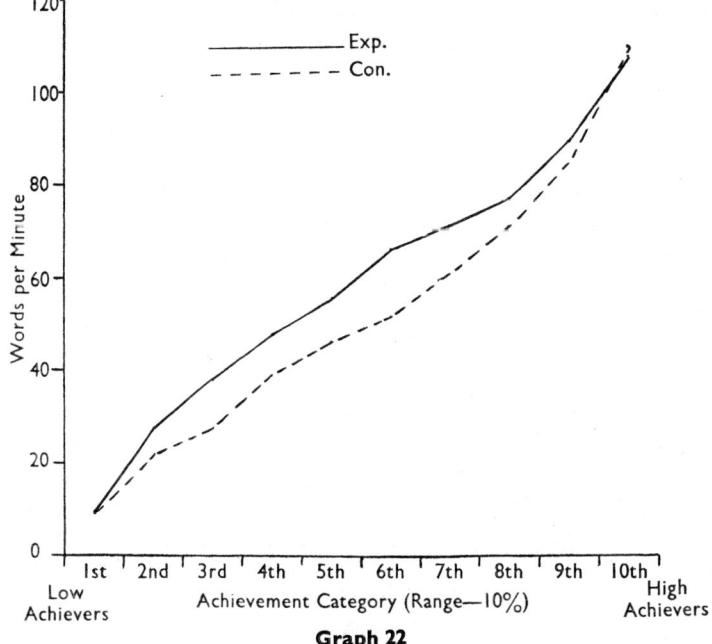

Neale Analysis (Form B) in t.o. to both groups over ten ranges of achievement
AFTER 3 YEARS — READING RATE

Graph 22

READING RATE SCORE IN t.o. OVER 10 RANGES OF ACHIEVEMENT
NEALE A — AFTER 1½ YEARS, NEALE B — AFTER 3 YEARS

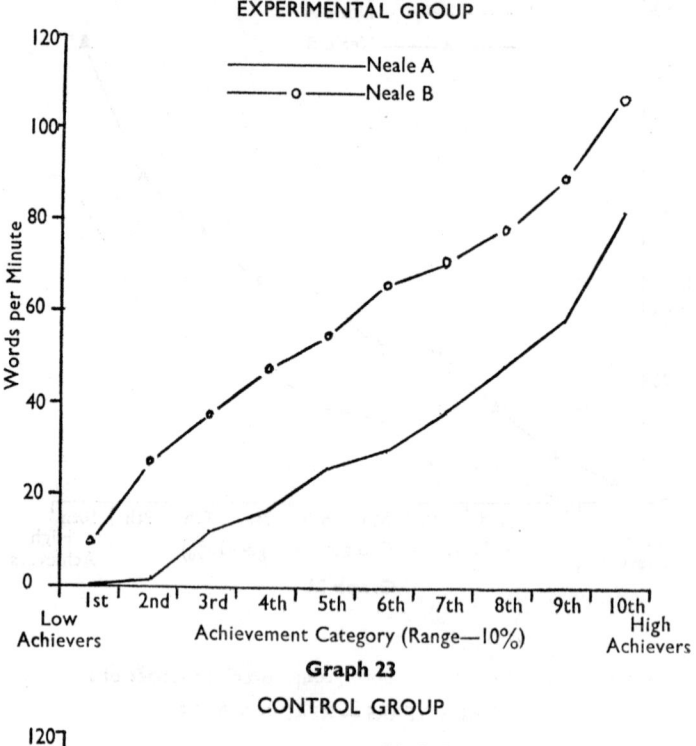

Graph 23

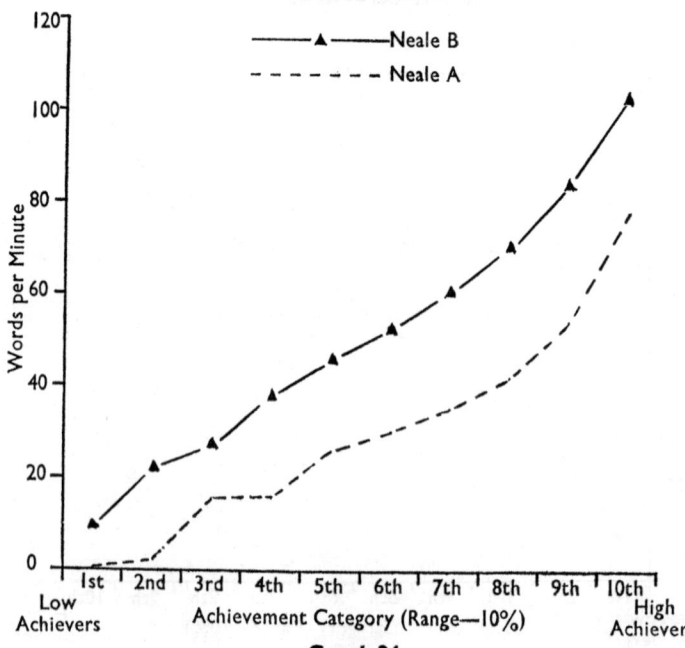

Graph 24

Neale Analysis (Form B) in t.o. to both groups over ten ranges of achievement
AFTER 3 YEARS — COMPREHENSION

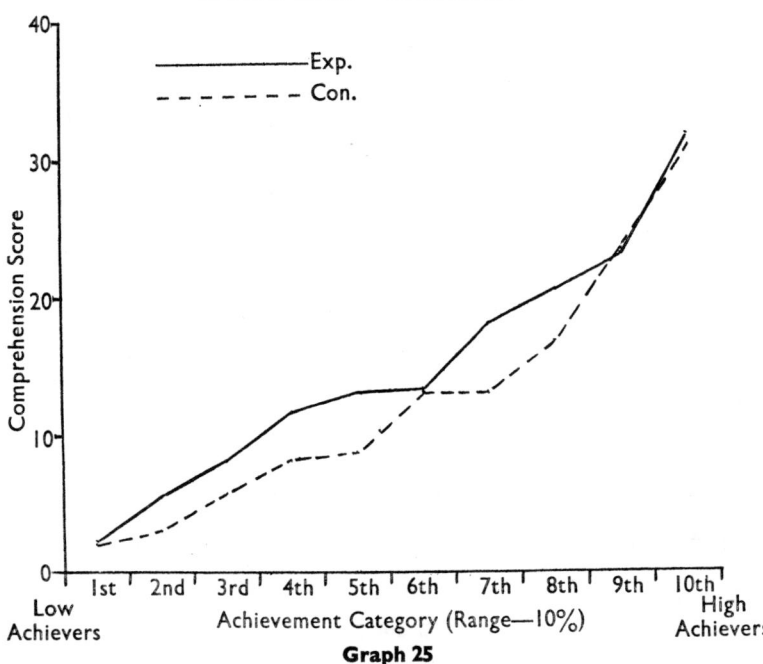

Graph 25

Experimental Group's Comprehension scores in t.o. over ten ranges of achievement
NEALE A — AFTER 1½ YEARS, NEALE B — AFTER 3 YEARS

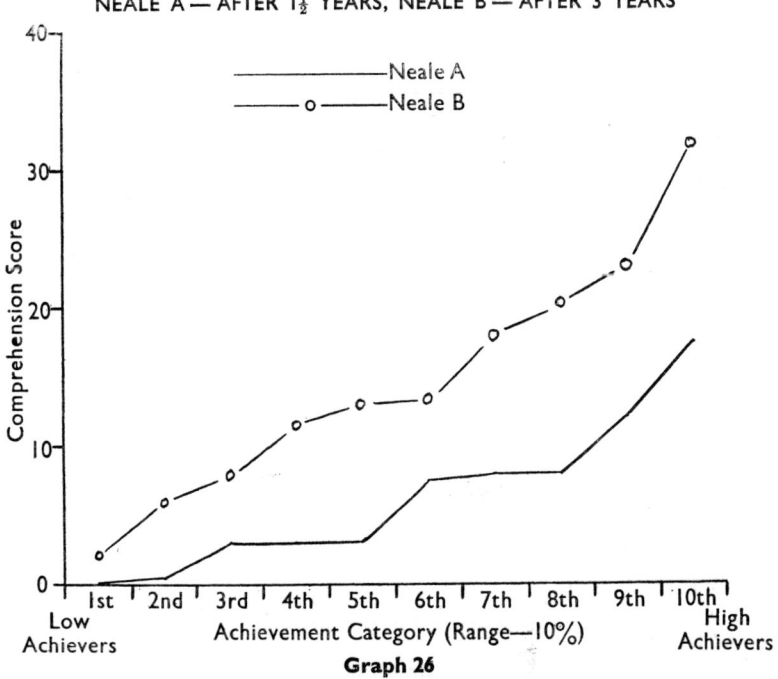

Graph 26

Control Group's Comprehension scores in t.o. over ten ranges of achievement
NEALE A — AFTER 1½ YEARS, NEALE B — AFTER 3 YEARS

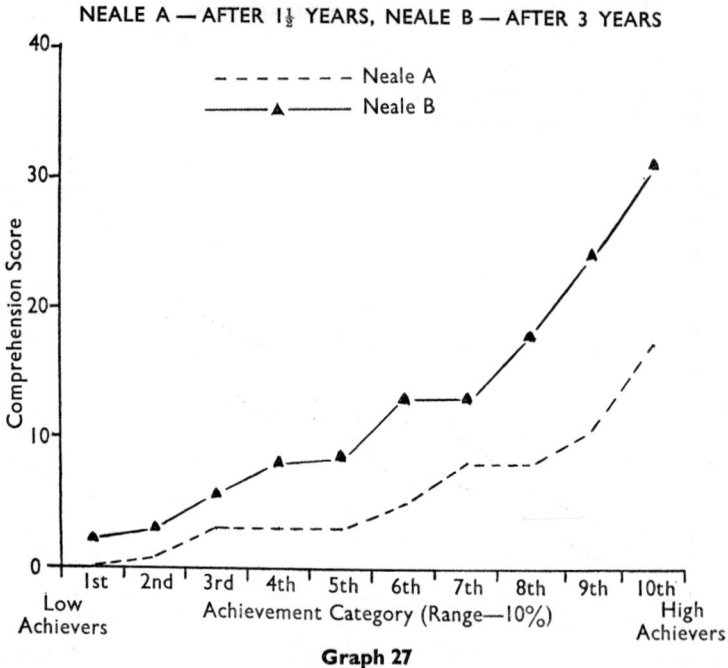

Graph 27

Scores on Schonell Graded Word Reading test (in t.o. to both groups) over ten ranges of achievement

AT BEGINNING OF 3rd YEAR

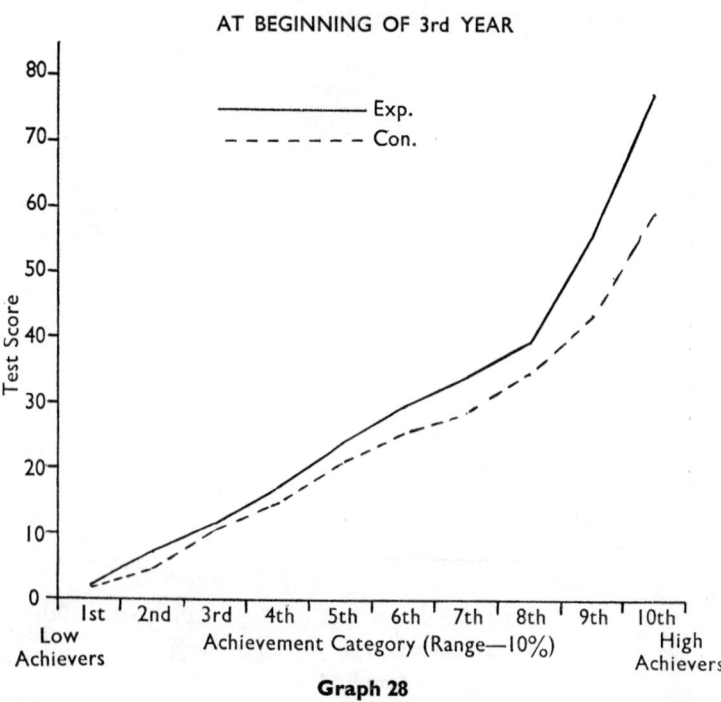

Graph 28

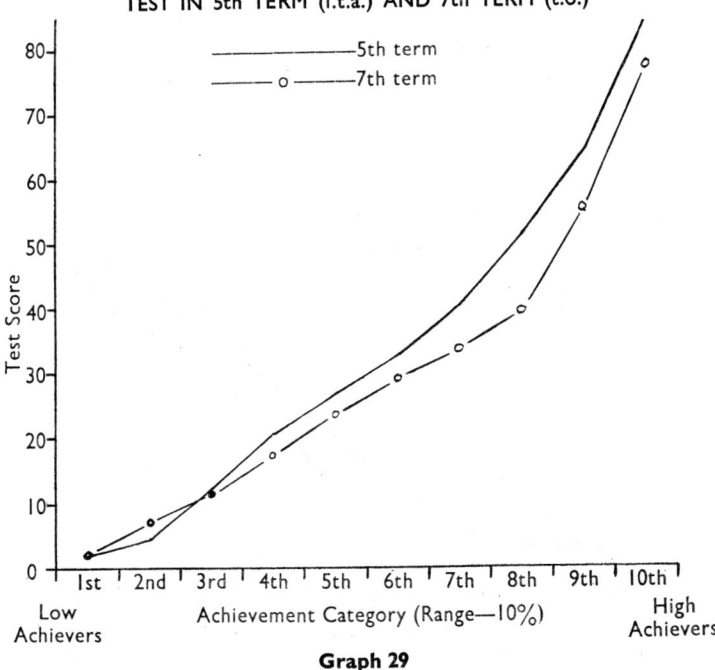

Graph 29

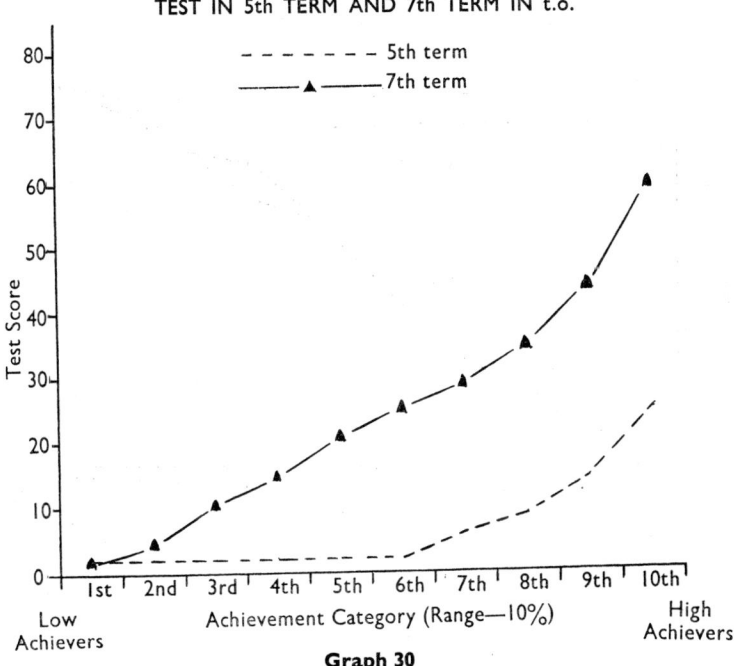

Graph 30

SILENT READING COMPREHENSION SCORES IN t.o. FOR BOTH GROUPS ON STANDISH N.S.45 TEST, OVER TEN RANGES OF ACHIEVEMENT

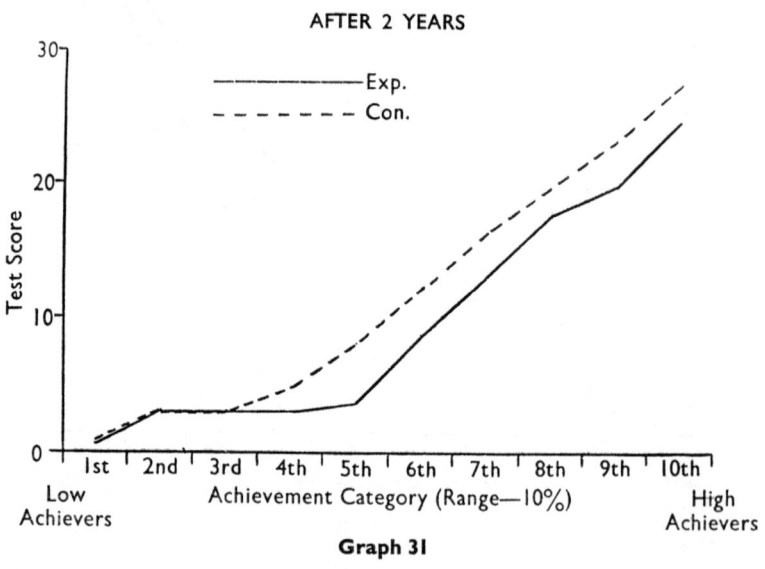

Graph 31

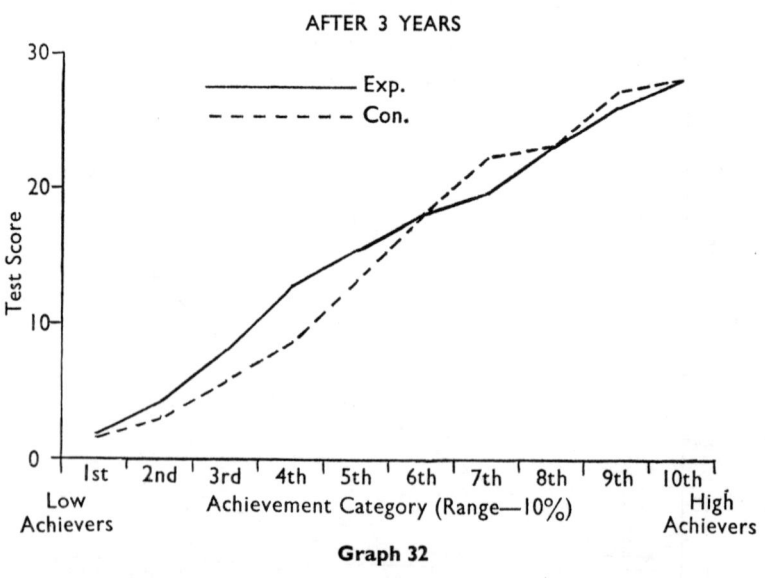

Graph 32

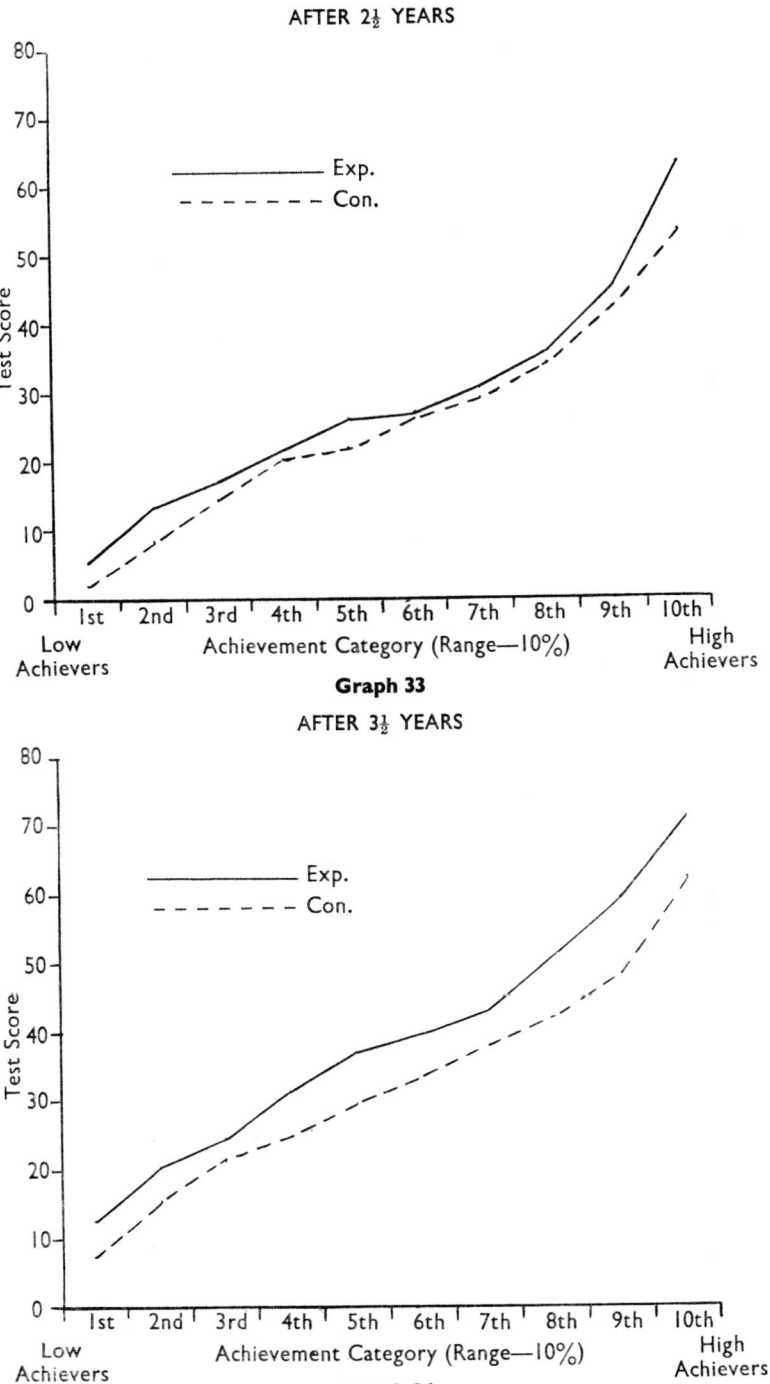

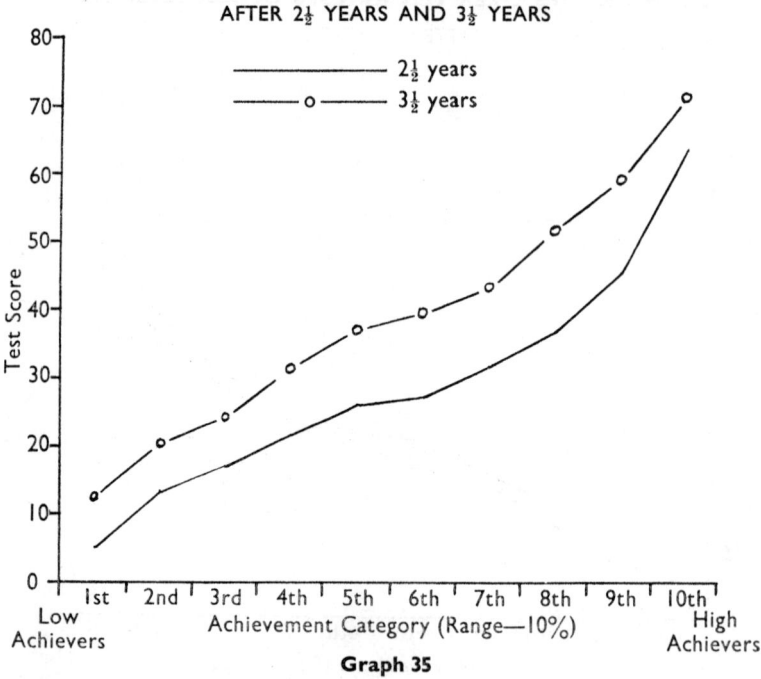

Graph 35

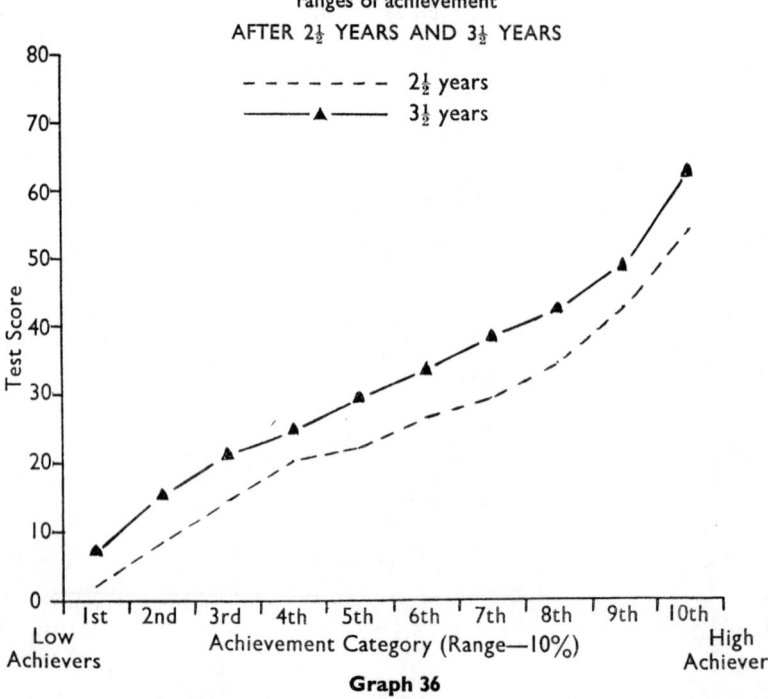

Graph 36

The Historical Background to the i.t.a. Research Report: a Selected Bibliography

BLOOMFIELD, L. and BARNHART, C. L. (1961). *Let's Read.* Detroit: Wayne State University Press.
BULLOKAR, W. (1580). *Booke at Large for the Amendment of English Orthographie.* London.
BURT, C. (1962). Preface in: DOWNING, J. A. (1962). tɷ bɛɛ *or not to be.* London: Cassell.
BURT, C., COOPER, W. F. and MARTIN, J. L. (1955). 'A psychological study of typography'. *British Journal of Statistical Psychology,* VIII, 29-58.
BUTLER, C. (1633). *English Grammar.* Oxford.
CARROLL, J. B. (1953). *The Study of Language.* Cambridge, Mass.: Harvard University Press.
CATTELL, J. Mck. (1885). 'Uber die Zeit der Erkennung und Berennung von Schriftzeichen, Bildern, und Farben'. *Philo. Stud.*, 2, 635-650.
CENTRAL ADVISORY COUNCIL FOR EDUCATION (1963). *Half Our Future: A Report.* London: H.M.S.O.
CHOU EN-LAI, WU YU-CHANG and LI CHIN-HSI (1958). *Reform of the Chinese Written Language.* Peking: Foreign Language Press.
CROCKETT, D. (1950). 'Towards More Rational Spelling'. M.Ed. thesis, Tufts College.
DAVIS, L. G. (1964). *K-a-t spelz cat: The New English Orthography.* New York: Carlton Press.
DOWNING, J. A. (1961). *How Your Children are Being Taught to Read with the Augmented Roman Alphabet* (subsequently retitled: *How Your Children are Being Taught to Read with the Initial Teaching Alphabet*). London: Reading Research Unit, University of London Institute of Education.
DOWNING, J. A. (1963). 'Is a "mental age of six" essential for "reading" readiness?' *Educational Research,* 6, 16-28.
DOWNING, J. A. (1964). *Examples of Children's Creative Writing from Schools using i.t.a.* London: Reading Research Unit, University of London Institute of Education.
DOWNING, J. A. (1964). *The Initial Teaching Alphabet.* London: Cassell; and New York: Macmillan.
DOWNING, J. A. (1965). *Interim Teachers' Manual for the Downing Readers.* London: Initial Teaching Publishing Company.
DOWNING, J. A. (1967). *Evaluating the Initial Teaching Alphabet.* London: Cassell.
DOWNING, J. A. and JONES, B. (1966). 'Some problems of evaluating i.t.a. A second experiment'. *Educational Research,* 8, 100-114.
DOWNING, J. A., FYFE, T. and LYON, M. (1967). 'The effects of the Initial Teaching Alphabet on young children's written composition'. *Educational Research,* 9, 2 (in press).
DURRELL, D. D. (1964). 'Learning Factors in Beginning Reading'. In: CUTTS, W. G. (ed.). *Teaching Young Children to Read:* Office of Education Bulletin No. 19. Washington, D.C.: U.S. Department of Health, Education and Welfare.

Research Report on the British Experiment with i.t.a.

ELKONIN, D. B. (1963). 'The psychology of mastering the elements of reading'. In: SIMON, B. and J. (eds.). *Educational Psychology in the U.S.S.R.* London: Routledge and Kegan Paul.

ELLIS, A. J. (1845). *A Plea for Phonotypy and Phonography.* Bath: Isaac Pitman Phonographic Institution.

ELLIS, A. J. (1848). *A Plea for Phonetic Spelling.* Bath: Pitman.

ELLIS, A. J. (1870). 'Spelling Difficulty and its Remedy, Glossic'. A lecture delivered to the College of Preceptors on 6 April 1870. London: *Phonetics —Language.*

ERDMANN, B. and DODGE, R. (1898). *Psychologische Untersuchungen über das Lesen auf Experimenteller Grundlage.* Halle: Neimeyer.

FARNHAM (1881). *The Sentence Method of Teaching Reading, Writing and Spelling, a Manual for Teachers.* Syracuse, N.Y.: C. W. Bardeen.

FEITELSON D. (1961). 'On the teaching of reading in non-European languages'. *English Language Teaching*, 16, 39-43.

FEITELSON, D. (1965). 'Structuring the teaching of reading according to major features of the language and its script'. *Elementary English*, 42, 870-877.

FRIES, C. C. (1962). *Linguistics and Reading.* New York: Holt, Rinehart and Winston.

FYFE, T. W. (1965). 'A Study of the Effects of the Initial Teaching Alphabet on Written Composition at Primary III Level'. Ed.B. thesis, University of St. Andrews.

GASPAR, R. (1964). 'The Prediction of Errors in the Reading of English on the Basis of Misleading Analogies in English Spelling'. M.A. thesis, University of London.

GATES, A. I. (1937). 'The necessary mental age for beginning reading'. *Elementary School Journal*, 37, 497-508.

GATTEGNO, C. (1962). *Words in Colour: Background and Principles.* Reading: Educational Explorers.

GATTEGNO, C. (1964). 'Words in colour'. *Forward Trends*, 8, 141-144.

GIBSON, E. J. (1965). 'Learning to read'. *Science*, 148, 1066-1072.

GLADSTONE, J. H. (1879). *Spelling Reform from an Educational Point of View.* London: Macmillan.

HARRISON, M. (1964). *Instant Reading.* London: Pitman.

HART, J. (1551). *The Opening of the Unreasonable Writing of our Inglish Toung.* London.

HART, J. (1569). *An Orthographie, conteyning the due order and reason, howe to write or paint thimage of manne's voice, moste like to the life or nature.* London.

HART, J. (1570). *A Methode or comfortable beginning for all unlearned, whereby they may bee taught to read English, in a very short time with pleasure.* London.

HODGES, R. (1644). *The English Primrose.* London.

HORN, E. (1929). 'The child's early experience with the letter *A*'. *Journal of Educational Psychology*, 20, 161-168.

JACKSON (1914). 'Phonetics and phonetic tests in the teaching of reading'. *Miscellanea Phonetica*, 1, 33-37.

JONES, B. (1966). 'An Attempt to Extend Control over Variables in a Second British Experiment with i.t.a.'. In: MAZURKIEWICZ, A. J. (ed.). *The Initial Teaching Alphabet and the World of English.* Hempstead, New York: Initial Teaching Alphabet Foundation.

A Selected Bibliography

JONES, J. K. (1965). 'Colour as an aid to visual perception in early reading'. *British Journal of Educational Psychology*, 35, 21-27.

KING, H. and PITMAN, I. J. (1960). 'Spelling—a handicap to reading?'. *Teachers World*, 26 February 1960.

LEE, W. R. (1960). *Spelling Irregularity and Reading Difficulty in English*. London: National Foundation for Educational Research in England and Wales.

LEIGH, T. (1966). *i.t.a. in the Classroom*. Edinburgh: Chambers.

MCBRIDE, F. (1965). *Teachers' Course in Writing with the Initial Teaching Alphabet*. London: Reading Research Unit, University of London Institute of Education.

MALMQUIST, E. (1964). *Overgang fran textning till vanlig skrivstil*. Stockholm: Kungl. Skoloverstyrelsen.

MARCH, F. A. (1893). *The Spelling Reform*. U.S. Bureau of Education, Circular of Information No. 8.

MASSACHUSETTS TEACHERS' ASSOCIATION (1853). 'Report on phonetics'. *Massachusetts Teacher*, 6, 25-28.

MINISTRY OF EDUCATION (1950). *Reading Ability*. (Pamphlet No. 18.) London: H.M.S.O.

MINISTRY OF EDUCATION (1957). *Standards of Reading—1948 to 1956*. (Pamphlet No. 32.) London: H.M.S.O.

MORRIS, J. M. (1959). *Reading in the Primary School*. London: Newnes.

PETERS, M. L. (1966). 'The Influence of Certain Reading Methods in the Spelling Ability of Junior School Children'. Abstract in: *Bulletin of the British Psychological Society*, Vol. 19, No. 62, 1966. Paper to appear in full in: *British Journal of Educational Psychology*, XXXVII, 1, February 1967.

PIAGET, J. and INHELDER, B. (1948). *La Representation de l'Espace chez l'Enfant*. Paris: Presses Universitaires de France.

PITMAN, I. J. (1959). 'Learning to read: a suggested experiment'. *The Times Educational Supplement*, 29 May 1959.

PITMAN, I. J. (1961). 'Learning to read: an experiment'. *Journal of the Royal Society of Arts*, 109, 149-180.

PITMAN, Sir James (1964). *The Assault on the Conventional Alphabets and Spelling*. Manchester: University of Manchester.

REED, W. J. (1960). *Spelling Reform and Our Schools*. Southampton: Simplified Spelling Society.

ST. LOUIS PUBLIC SCHOOLS (1869). *Fifteenth Annual Report of the Board of Directors*, 95-98.

ST. LOUIS PUBLIC SCHOOLS (1871). *Seventeenth Annual Report of the Board of Directors*, 133-134 and 182.

ST. LOUIS PUBLIC SCHOOLS (1872). *Eighteenth Annual Report of the Board of Directors*.

SHAW, B. (1906). Letter to *The Times*, 25 September 1906.

SHAW, B. (1946). Letter to *Tit-Bits*, 22 March 1946.

SHELDON, W. (1964). 'The Initial Teaching Alphabet'. *Grade Teacher*, October 1964, 34, 118 and 130.

SIMPLIFIED SPELLING SOCIETY (1924). *The Best Method of Teaching Children to Read and Write*. London: Pitman.

SMITH, Sir T. (1568). *De recta et emendata Linguae Anglicae Scriptione Dialogus*. Paris.

SOFFIETTI, J. P. (1955). 'Why children fail to read: a linguistic analysis'. *Harvard Educational Review*, 25, 63-84.

SOUTHGATE, V. (1963). 'Augmented Roman Alphabet experiment. An outsider's report'. *Educational Review*, 16, 32-41.
STOTT, D. H. (1965). *Roads to Literacy*. Glasgow: Holmes.
TAUBER (1958). 'Spelling Reform in the United States'. Ph.D. thesis, Columbia University.
VERNON, M. D. (1957). *Backwardness in Reading*. Cambridge: Cambridge University Press.
VIKAINEN, I. (1965). *A Diagnosis of Specific Backwardness in Spelling*. Turku (Finland): University of Turku Institute of Education.
WIJK, A. (1958). *Regularized English*. Stockholm: Wiksell.
WIJK, A. (1960). *'gae, foot, dee' spells gwd*. Distribution: A. B. Seelig, Stockholm.
ZEITZ, F. (1966). 'Unifon—the Sound Alphabet'. *School and Community*, April, p. 23.

Evaluations

Evaluations—1

A. STERL ARTLEY
Professor of Education, University of Missouri.

THE Downing report presents the results of a definitive and completely objective study of the value of the Initial Teaching Alphabet in early reading. Though studies of its use elsewhere may show results at variance with those obtained in England and Wales it is hoped that such results would be obtained from studies done with the degree of objectivity found in this.

Two questions may be asked by anyone contemplating the use of a code system that regularizes the phoneme-grapheme relationship, whether that system is i.t.a. or any one of several others that are being discussed currently in the literature. The first question may be stated as follows: Does evidence exist to show that English orthography is a deterrent to learning to read? In other words, is the irregular and inconsistent English orthography a factor that must be reckoned with in early reading instruction, either to be accepted for what it is or to be circumvented in one way or another?

To this question we seem to have a definitive answer from the Downing study. It is a deterring factor. In terms of rate of progress and extent of achievement the children who were taught with the transitional writing medium made greater progress than those taught through the use of the traditional orthographic system. Downing answers the first question in these words: 'The unequivocal conclusion from the results of these experiments is that the traditional orthography of English is an important cause of difficulty in teaching and learning reading and writing in English-speaking countries.'

With an answer to the first question being positive, the second naturally follows: Does a teaching alphabet that regularizes the phoneme-grapheme relationship remove the spelling impediment and thereby facilitate learning to read? Though not providing an unequivocal answer to this question, the study gives a strong indication that it does. Downing shows that though there is an initial impairment in reading ability during transfer from i.t.a. to t.o., and for a short time thereafter, by the end of the third year the i.t.a. groups show superiority in word recognition, reading accuracy, speed and comprehension (Neale test). In terms of the results from the Standish test, however, the results are less clear, for after two years of instruction those children who had been taught with the words spelled conventionally tended to be superior to those taught with words spelled with the i.t.a. characters. At the end of three years the trend was reversed and the results showed slight superiority for the i.t.a. taught children. However, in neither case were the differences statistically significant. It might be pointed out in relation to the above comparisons that possibly the Standish test would be more nearly similar to those used to measure reading achievement in the United States, since it is a silent reading test. The Neale test, on the other hand, measures reading accuracy, speed, and comprehension in an oral manner.

Once it has been established that the English orthography is a road-block to learning to read, and that this road-block may be removed by a code system that regularizes the phoneme-grapheme relationship, a third question stands in need of an answer. Is the Initial Teaching Alphabet the best code system available? To this question the Downing study gives us no answer, nor was it designed to do so.

It is important to point out, as does Downing, that the i.t.a. is an *ad hoc* system, the assumption being that changes would be made in the system as indicated through research. Indeed, it would be extremely unfortunate if at this stage in the development of the Initial Teaching Alphabet, it were to be assumed that both the code system and the method of its use were fixed and established so that no further work on either would be necessary. Were this to take place the chances would be great that we would be operating with something less than the best. This, the teaching profession could hardly condone.

Downing points out several areas in need of research. Based on linguistic studies and the experience of those who have used the alphabet, an examination should be made of the characters themselves in terms of number and formation. Seemingly, from this study there are problems encountered by children at the transfer stage that might be alleviated if changes were made either in the characters or spelling principles. As Downing says there is need to consider the design of the transition system itself so as ' . . . to maximize the combined effects of simplicity and regularity at the beginning stage and similarity to t.o. on the relevant dimensions for the transition stage.'

Certainly a look should be given to the principles and rules for indicating phonemes with i.t.a. characters. It would be a mistake to establish rules that would make it difficult to indicate speech sounds as they were actually spoken and heard in various regions. If the Initial Teaching Alphabet is to have practical use it should not be considered a means to regularize pronunciation.

The mode of transfer from i.t.a. to t.o. should be subjected to careful analysis in an attempt to prevent possible retardation in reading progress during the transfer stage. Is it possible that transfer should be made earlier than was attempted in these studies? Could the learners have become so habituated to the i.t.a. orthography that the 'unlearning' process slowed reading progress? Our preliminary studies in the use of i.t.a. with adult illiterates indicate that there is value in pointing out similarities and differences between words written in i.t.a. and the same words written in t.o. on very early levels. Thus, in a sense, the learner is making gradual and almost unconscious transfer to t.o. from the very outset. Whether or not a modification of this approach would work with young children is an interesting question.

Even after the alphabet has been scrutinized in the light of the best linguistic, psychological, and pedagogical analysis, it should then be compared with other approaches and media designed to overcome the irregularities of conventional English spelling. At this time it would be unfortunate if the Initial Teaching Alphabet were to become a cult. If it does, an idea with promise might soon have its demise.

Evaluations—2

SIR CYRIL BURT
Emeritus Professor, University of London

MOST practical suggestions for dealing with current educational problems seem at the present time to arouse heated discussions in the popular press, on television and on radio, and even at professional conferences; and the proposal to introduce a reformed type of alphabet in order to facilitate the teaching of reading has proved no exception. In the past, a wide variety of ingenious schemes with similar aims in view have been put forward; but, certainly during my own lifetime, none of the many suggestions advocated by psychologists, by linguists, or by teachers themselves has ever aroused either so much interest or such vigorous criticism as the introduction of Sir James Pitman's Augmented Roman Alphabet.

In the early stages the enthusiasm of both supporters and opponents did much to facilitate the institution of an elaborate series of researches into the problems raised: teachers and educational officials were both eager to see the new medium tried out in actual practice. But in the later phases of the inquiry the emotional propaganda both for and against has tended rather to obscure the real nature of the proposal as well as its apparent advantages and defects. It is to be hoped that the present publication of the data so far obtained and the symposium of comments which accompanies them will help those concerned with the teaching of reading to arrive at unprejudiced and impartial conclusions for themselves.

As a member of the committee formed to initiate and guide the project I was asked to contribute a preface to Downing's first publication on the subject tɷ beε *or not to be: The New Augmented Roman Alphabet Explained and Illustrated* (1962). I then mentioned the many hidden difficulties which all experimental researches of this type have to meet; and, on the basis of past experience, I pointed out that 'almost invariably in a scientific investigation, when one sets out to confirm or confute some plausible proposal, the outcome is seldom the plain straightforward "yes" or "no" that cross-examining counsel love to demand: usually it appears that there are elements of truth in both the opposing views, and more often than not the most rewarding results are the discoveries made by the way: fresh problems, quite unforeseen, nearly always emerge, and new facts, quite unexpected, are vividly brought to light'. Downing now tells us (1966)[1] that 'four years later we at the Reading Research Unit are in the thick of the new problems' thus predicted. If the ultra-cautious reader of this volume still feels that none of the advantages tentatively hoped for at the outset have as yet been proved, he must at least agree that the elaborate investigations here described have been entirely worth while. No one can read the preceding report without recognizing that we now know far more about the processes of reading and of learning to read than we did before the experiments were undertaken, and that valuable experience has been gained in regard to the practicable methods of research in the bewildering field of education.

The results reported in this volume relate to the first series of experiments planned and started in 1961. This was from the outset envisaged as a longitudinal study; and for a final evaluation we should, I think, still wait until the pupils concerned have approached nearer to the end of their school careers. Not for another year or two will it be possible to publish a survey of their actual attainments after fully completing the change from the initial teaching alphabets to traditional orthography. Meanwhile, profiting by the experience earned in this first attempt, Downing embarked on a second set of experiments in 1963, which, it is hoped, will meet some of the doubts and criticisms aroused by the earlier inquiries. A preliminary report has been published in *Educational Research*, VIII, 1966, pp.100-114.

When planning the first set of investigations, Downing resolved to adhere to the conditions of a 'field experiment': that is to say, instead of arranging the artificial conditions which psychologists commonly impose when carrying out a formal laboratory test, he decided to keep as closely as possible to the everyday situation of the ordinary classroom, and to 'follow a programme of evaluation which should be immediately meaningful to teachers and administrators'. This entailed sacrificing some of the more rigorous requirements of an ideal experimental and statistical research; but, in dealing with a practical problem of this type, it was, in my view, the correct policy to follow. Before time, trouble, and money could be spent on a more refined and carefully controlled investigation, the first essential was to secure concrete and detailed evidence to show whether or not there was at least a *prima facie* case that the advantages expected from the new teaching-method might be fulfilled.

[1] *Educational Research*, *VIII*, 1966, p. 100.

The i.t.a. Symposium

Bearing these limitations clearly in mind, let us now briefly glance at the main results of the experiments so far as they take us at the present time. In the past, those who have put forward propaganda for the reform of English spelling have commonly assumed that there was a need for a complete and permanent change from the present irregular orthography with its inadequate alphabet to an augmented but simplified alphabet and a consistent and regularized mode of spelling. The principles adopted by Sir James Pitman were quite different. What he contemplated was merely an initial teaching alphabet, expressly designed as a 'transitional writing system', not a perfect scheme of purely phonetic spelling. The intention was merely that the new alphabet should form an introductory device, to be used by beginners during the earliest stages of learning to read, and to be exchanged at a later date for the old traditional system. Many critics of this proposal have entirely overlooked the fact that his object was, not the familiar notion of a complete spelling reform, but simply a transitional teaching device.

In assessing the value of any such proposal it is clear that two distinct questions must be answered. (1) Assuming that the numerous irregularities of the traditional orthography greatly increase the difficulties encountered by the child when learning to read, do the experimental results suffice to demonstrate that with a new and regularized method of printing children learn to read far more successfully? (2) Granted that the innovation does increase the children's success so long as they are working with the new material, is there any evidence to show that it also increases their success when eventually they change over to the conventional mode of printing? Is it not perhaps more likely that they will have by then become so habituated to the modified style that they will experience even greater difficulty when they are required to read ordinary print and to spell in the ordinary way? They will, it might be thought, not merely have to learn a new and unfamiliar orthography, but also to unlearn the familiar.

Downing's method of answering these questions is to take matched groups of beginners and arrange for one group to be taught with the old style of spelling and the other by the modified procedure. He then applies statistical tests for accuracy, speed, and comprehension of reading and for correctness of spelling, and compares the marks obtained by each group first in the earlier stages while the experimental group is still using the novel material, and again when the experimental group has changed over to the traditional mode of printing. This is supplemented by a series of graphs comparing the

Evaluations

two groups in terms of ten 'achievement categories' or grades. Now in considering the conclusions to be drawn from these statistical results, I have to confess to an antecedent prejudice of my own. From the work that I myself have done, when studying methods of teaching, particularly methods of teaching the young beginner to read, I have become convinced that the individual differences between one child and another are so great and so numerous that it is, as a rule, decidedly precarious to draw any generalizations relating to children as a whole. The mere comparison of group-differences may easily be misleading. Thus, imagine for simplicity that it is possible to train the same child by both methods and let us suppose that in a class of 20 children 15 lose on an average one mark when taught by the new medium and that the other 5 gain on an average 4 marks: then, if we compared the two means, we might be tempted to conclude that the children in general improved when taught by the new procedure; whereas the true conclusion would be that the majority were handicapped and only a small number actually benefited.[1]

Most of us, when we read, pay no attention to the spelling unless it is faulty: the general look of the visible word or the phrase, taken as a whole, directly suggests its meaning without any analysis into letters or sounds. Many children, particularly those who are visualizers, learn to read in this way from the very start. Indeed, several educational psychologists have argued that this is the most sensible way to learn the commoner words, which also happen to include the chief irregular words. Some children, however, seem almost devoid of visual imagery. Of these many are audiles; and their natual method of tackling a new word is to translate it letter by letter in to its component sounds. There is, however, a third type of child, less commonly recognized—the motile. For him, what the teacher calls 'sounds' are really the movements needed to produce the sounds, or the 'mental images' of such movements. It is, one might suspect, chiefly the children of these last two types who

---

[1] Something of this sort (though of course by no means so extreme) seems discernible in Downing's graphs for successive 'categories' or grades. Here the inferences I should draw from 'inspection of the graphs' would, I think, differ from those that he suggests. Consequently, we must wait for the more detailed discussion which (he tells us) he is publishing elsewhere, and which will presumably supply tests of significance. However, the individual differences which I have chiefly in mind are those resulting from differences in mental abilities rather than in 'categories of achievement', and particularly *special* abilities (differences in visual and auditory perception, in mechanical memory, in mental imagery, etc.).

could profit most by the regularized orthography. Extreme or pure types, however, are rare: the majority are of a mixed type, though usually one of the three main forms predominates. Accordingly, what the pyschologist would like to know is which are the various silent modes of learning that different individuals usually adopt when dealing with material printed either in the ordinary way or in the modified orthography.

There is one further limitation in this comparison of means. The first question put by the statistical critic, with his demand for rigorous proof, is—whether or not the differences observed could be ascribed to chance, or, as he would say, to the mere effects of random sampling. Downing, therefore, quite properly proceeds to assess what is termed the 'significance' of the various differences between the means. By this term is meant the *statistical* significance: but the ordinary reader is apt to interpret it as implying *practical* significance. By comparing very large samples, quite small and unimportant differences can be shown to be 'significant' in the statistical sense. Taking samples as large as those compared by Downing one can easily demonstrate that the difference in height between scholarship winners and those who fail is statistically significant: but no one would think of selecting a candidate and measuring his height simply because the average scholarship winner is a fifth of an inch taller than the average failure.[1]

In his first book on the new alphabet, Downing describes how he tested two groups of bright children who were extremely backward in reading: we are told that 'at the end of eight weeks of teaching

---

[1] In testing the significance of the differences between the means of the two groups, Downing (rather surprisingly) has not followed the regular procedure (calculating the standard error for each difference), but instead has adapted the Kolmogorov-Smirnov test. This test, however, was first put forward as a highly sensitive test 'for *any* kind of difference in the two distributions'. It attempts to do so by converting each to a two-fold distribution, and choosing that particular distribution which will yield re-scaled means with a maximum difference. The problem envisaged is therefore different from that of Downing; and, as actual calculation quickly shows, the method is apt to ascribe significance to a relatively small difference which would be rejected as non-significant by the customary procedure. But the whole problem is complicated by the fact that most of the scholastic tests adopted prove to have been rather too difficult for these particular groups, and as a result the distributions, instead of conforming approximately to the normal type, are badly skewed. In his second series he attempts to correct for skewness by a logarithmic transformation; but, instead of deducing an appropriate equation for each table, he takes logarithms of the marks as they stand — a decidedly rough and naive procedure.

Evaluations

(with the two different alphabets) the children's reading ability was tested on the Burt Graded Reading Test' (transliterated for the experimental group). The average of the experimental group was 27.6 words, that of the control group only 11.0—a difference of nearly 18 words. The test is so graded that there are 10 words for each successive age: the improvement was therefore equivalent to a progress of nearly two years over that achieved by the children taught with the 'traditional spelling'. In his present report, however, Downing usually is content to demonstrate that the differences found are statistically significant, without going on to indicate what precisely is the nature and the magnitude of the difference in concrete practical terms.

He states the conclusions he hopes to prove in the form of seven succinct propositions. With some slight simplifications in wording they are as follows:

1. Children taught by the initial teaching alphabet, i.e. those in the experimental group, should advance more rapidly to the harder types of reading book. From the relevant table (E1) we learn that after $2\frac{1}{2}$ years, 78 per cent. of the experimental group, but only 38 per cent. of the control group have got beyond Book V. Roughly speaking, it would seem that those taught by the new method were more than one book ahead. To the teacher this result, I think, gives the clearest picture of the success attained.

2. Children in the experimental group should achieve higher scores on standardized reading tests. This provides a more rigorous comparison. On turning to the tables (E2) we find that, with the Schonell word test (administered after about $1\frac{1}{2}$ years in school), the average for the experimental group was 34 words out of a 100, and that for the control group barely 15 words. With the Neale tests for accuracy, speed, and comprehension, the differences were similar but much smaller. In the later experiment, where more strenuous efforts were made to reduce what Downing calls the Hawthorne Effect, the results were not quite so clear. With the 'first Schonell test' the control group at one of the thirteen schools achieved a much better average than the experimental group; at only two of the schools was the performance of the experimental group significantly superior. With the 'second Schonell test' all the seven differences which were statistically significant were in favour of the experimental group, but with six schools there was no significant difference. With the Neale tests the differences were statistically significant only in the case of three schools (for accuracy) and two (for speed and comprehension). Downing tells us that he

proposes to investigate 'why the superiority of the i.t.a. results is less marked than in the original experiment'.[1]

3. Provided they have become fluent with the transitional alphabet, the achievements of the experimental group, after changing to the traditional orthography, should not be inferior to their achievements with the transitional alphabet. Judging by the tables, this seems true in regard to speed; indeed their performance with the t.o. test was actually better than their performance with the i.t.a. test which they took a month earlier. But with accuracy and comprehension their performance with traditional spelling was inferior, as indeed, I think, one would expect. The difficulties seem to arise chiefly over words in which the visible word-pattern is markedly different with the two methods of spelling.

4. After the change, pupils in the experimental group should read material in traditional spelling with greater speed, accuracy, and comprehension than pupils taught with the traditional orthography from the very outset. Here we learn that although the experimental group achieved superior scores on all three measures when tested in the middle of the second school year, the improvement was too small to be statistically significant. In the second experiment we learn that 'the overall comparison is slightly, though not significantly, in favour of pupils taught throughout with the traditional orthography'. In this case, however, we are told that, as assessed a month before the test was taken, many of the children had not in fact actually completed the change. It would perhaps be instructive if Downing could add a note giving results for those who had been 'transferred to t.o. by their teachers'.

5. After the change to the traditional orthography the spelling of the experimental group should be superior to that of the control group. The results obtained with a standardized spelling test reveal a slight superiority, non-significant in the third school year but fully significant in the fourth.

6. and 7. The written vocabulary of the experimental group should be more extensive, and their written compositions longer, than those of the control group. On the whole, after making due allowances for the difficulties in assessing these two criteria, Downing concludes that 'there is a clear tendency for i.t.a. to give superior results'.

Before attempting to estimate the net results of all these experiments, there is one further problem to be faced. In the past, whenever any

[1] DOWNING, J. and JONES, B. (1966). 'Some problems of evaluating i.t.a. A second experiment'. Educational Research, Vol. VIII, No. 2, see p. 113.

Evaluations

novel method of teaching children to read has been introduced and tested along the lines adopted here, the first results almost invariably show that the performance of the group taught by the new method tends to be superior to the performance of the group taught by the old familiar procedure. The teachers who volunteer to try the new method are often persons with a fervid belief in its merits and keen to demonstrate its superiority. The children's interest is excited by the change from the ordinary humdrum routine. With the present inquiry the visits from educationists, journalists, radio and television producers threw a good deal of extra limelight on the experimental group, and so introduced a further exciting factor.

Downing has been fully alive to these irrelevant influences, and has done his best to eliminate their occurrence or allow for their effects in assessing the results. This is particularly the case with the second set of experiments planned a few years ago. Nevertheless, as he himself candidly admits, the measures so far taken, and the supplementary arguments employed, are not altogether convincing. My own suggestion would be that the control group should itself be converted into an alternative experimental group: e.g. while the material used should still be printed in the traditional style, there should be some novel change in the teaching methods; the teachers in charge should be enthusiastic for some special teaching technique—phonic, look-and-say, or an ingenious mixture; or the reading material, though preserving the usual spelling, might embody some of the supplementary devices which many teachers would favour—e.g. the use of differently coloured letters or of diacritical signs.

Instead of the Kolmogorov-Smirnov test of statistical significance, which Downing acknowledges is not entirely satisfactory, I should prefer to adopt an analysis of variance, and, with that procedure in view, to arrange the groups by strictly random assignments in accordance with the principles of the so-called 'Latin square'. Complicated as it appears, this plan proves quite feasible in practice, as I sought to show in a study of reading methods (alphabetic, phonic, and the like) which I myself carried out some years ago.[1]

Meanwhile, I think we can safely draw two main conclusions. First, whether or not the new method is likely to prove beneficial for children generally, there is strong evidence to show that it possesses

---

[1] 'Teaching backward readers', *Brit. J. Educ. Psychol.*, XVI, 1946, pp. 116-132. A readily accessible account will be found in: WALKER, H. M., and LEV, J. (1953). *Statistical Inference*. New York: Holt; London: Constable (pp. 348-360).

The i.t.a. Symposium

marked advantages for pupils of certain types—probably, I would suspect, for the audiles and the motiles and particularly for those of superior intelligence: (for the visualizers and for the dull and backward generally its merits are in my view open to doubt). Secondly, and still more important, Downing has made a clear and convincing case for further and still more elaborate researches in the schools into the various problems thus raised. If the investigation is repeated, at least two changes should be made: first, the tests employed should be more appropriate to the level of the children tested; secondly, both in the preliminary planning and in the final analysis of the results the advice of an experienced statistician should be obtained. As it is, the methods of comparison here adopted are far too crude and naive to carry conviction with a critical reader, particularly since many of the crucial differences prove to be so small that their statistical significance seems highly questionable.

Evaluations—3

HUNTER DIACK
Senior Tutor, Institute of Education, University of Nottingham

I am not aware of any fully-detailed research which has shown the old alphabetic or 'spelling' method of teaching children to read to be superior to other systems, but all other systems have frequently been shown by statistical investigation to be superior to one another with varying degrees of authority. The reason why the alphabetic method stands apart is purely, I think, because, in English-speaking countries, it had gone out before statistics came in; otherwise it would have been as much the subject of scientific research as any of the other methods that have been put forward.

The reason why reading methods are so malleable under statistical treatment is to be found in the presence of a large number of variables, in any experimental situation where children's reading is being studied. When J. C. Daniels and I were comparing groups of children in infant schools, we felt it necessary to use the rateable value of the houses owned or occupied by the children's parents as a means of obtaining comparable populations, but all the time we were very much aware of how remote the individual child became during the statistical treatment of the results.

Downing can fairly claim that in his investigations he has taken every possible factor into account and dealt with each one in the most careful statistical fashion. I have no doubt that other contributors to this symposium will give due attention to the statistical aspects of his work. My interest lies in a different direction. Indeed, though I do not see very well what else he could have done, I think it is a pity that quite so much of Downing's time and energy have had to be devoted to the statistical assessment of his results. This concentration of his energies has, I feel, led him to neglect other aspects of the teaching of reading. Nor am I at all sure that the line he followed really gives the answer to the question as to whether i.t.a. is the best solution to our reading problems.

If we accept the most favourable statistics put forward by Downing, the most we can say is that children taught to read by means of an i.t.a. version of the *Janet and John* readers made better progress than comparable children taught by means of the *Janet and John* readers in the normal t.o. version. That is to say, children taught by means of a series of readers which does not recognize the alphabetic principle at the earlier stages of reading do not progress so well as comparable children taught by the same readers transcribed in such a way that nowhere are they remote from the alphabetic principle.

If we accept the superiority of i.t.a. as proved in this context, can we go further and say that therefore any children taught by means of i.t.a. books will be superior to comparable children taught by means of books in traditional orthography? To do so would, I think, be stretching logic too far.

It may well be thought that, since I am co-author of a series of readers that are phonically graded, there is a vested interest behind those few sentences. I do not, however, feel that this weighs at all heavily with me; the experience of teachers over the past twelve years or so seems to indicate that that particular phonically graded scheme, the *Royal Road Readers*, fits in better with later remedial work than in the infant school, owing to the manner of its design.

What would have happened, however, if Downing had designed phonically graded material to be used along with i.t.a. instead of the extreme 'Look and say' readers which he did use? There would have been no experiment at the early stages because the two sets of material would have been identical! The interesting thing to see, if such an experiment is yet carried out, would be whether the two sets of children, whose progress at the early stages would by the nature of things be the same, would show divergent progress when the stage of introducing phonic irregularities was reached. The i.t.a. children would then have the advantage of regular spelling while the t.o. children would have the well-known illogicalities of English spelling to deal with. By the time they had reached that stage, however, many of the i.t.a. children would be ready for transfer to t.o. and so the experiment would be in danger of foundering.

It seems, therefore, that in order to keep an experiment in being at all, Downing had to use the strongly contrasting material available from the two versions of *Janet and John*. In so doing, however, he was limiting the deductions that can logically be drawn from his results. There is in fact, however great the weight of statistical evidence, no logical basis for saying that i.t.a. is a more efficient means than any other for teaching children to read English. One can only point to a certain superiority over children taught by means of 'look and say' material.

Earlier in this article I said that Downing's attention was drawn away from some important aspects of the reading problem. The one that interests me most is the perception of words by children. Since print is speech made visible, it seems to me that one of the most important aspects of the study of children learning to read is how they perceive words.

On this topic Downing has nothing to say whatsoever. Misreadings are certainly quoted but there is a notable lack of discussion of the processes of perception that lie behind such mis-readings.

This points to the extreme thinness of the research. We may admit that the more limited in intention a piece of research is, the more water-tight its results will be; but here we have an investigation of considerable size which in the end boils down to the statement that *bus* and *animal* are easier words to reach than *dough* and *aeroplane*, or (to put it in another way) that a regularly spelt language offers fewer difficulties than an irregularly spelt one. This, of course, is not the whole story: the rest consists of the statement that if you turn all the words into regular spelling the children will still have gained even if the words are turned back again to irregular spelling.

There is one reason why I welcome Downing's report and welcome the amount of attention given to i.t.a.: it is that I feel that anything which works in any way towards improving the system of spelling in English is to be welcomed. There may be growing up a generation less hide-bound in this respect. On the other hand I find it regrettable that the research has been carried on in such a limited way. It seems to me a pity that such facile methods of persuading teachers have been adopted. Again and again it has been argued in favour of i.t.a. that a teacher need not change her methods—only the material needs to be changed, from t.o. to i.t.a. This is as much as to say the teacher need not change her ideas, that no re-thinking about the teaching of reading is necessary, only the introduction of a new kind of print. Everything else remains the same.

I should have hoped for something more fundamental than that, but perhaps it is still to come.

Evaluations—4

R. GULLIFORD
Senior Lecturer, Department of Education, University of Birmingham

WHEN volunteer schools were sought for the first i.t.a. experiments, teachers were reluctant to come forward—no doubt being reluctant to hazard their pupils' progress with a new medium. i.t.a. research and the experience of teachers using it routinely in the schools have provided clear evidence on at least some points: that children can learn to read without difficulty through the use of i.t.a.; that teachers can adapt their usual teaching methods to it easily; that—slow learners excepted—children appear to proceed more rapidly through the early stages of learning to read and that the transition which many thought would present problems occurs without undue difficulty though, as this report shows, there are some transfer problems which need further study. I would predict that i.t.a. has come to stay. Even if it were not to be widely used in the beginning stages of reading, I think it would continue to be used as one approach in the repertoire of remedial teachers of older backward children, with whom a novel approach is so often needed for the re-teaching of pupils who have consistently failed. The i.t.a. experiments may also have drawn attention, as Downing suggests, to other ways of circumventing the irregularities of t.o. Indeed, the trend towards a more careful and systematic development of phonics instruction was apparent before the introduction of i.t.a. To reduce unnecessary difficulties in learning to read at the early stages is a rational and economical thing to do; whether it would be sensible and economical in the long term to encourage large scale use of i.t.a. is another matter and in my view awaits further evidence.

This rather neutral attitude is based on a realization of the complex of factors which underlies the learning and teaching of reading in our schools, and that the matter of a regularized spelling is but one of them. I think it is important that anyone considering the use of i.t.a. should not simply focus on the problems presented by traditional orthography but should consider the process of learning to read as a whole, the wide range of problems presented by pupils, and problems concerned with the organization of reading instruction n schools.

Evaluations

The first point to be made is an elementary one, but one which nevertheless should be stated lest it be overlooked. i.t.a. is not a method of teaching reading; it is a system of regularized spelling. The word 'method' in connection with reading is often reduced in meaning. It is often, for example, reduced to an unreal argument about 'Look and say' and phonic methods. The argument can only be about the relative use which is made of visual, phonic, kinaesthetic, contextual and other cues at different stages of teaching reading. An effective teacher has thought out, or worked out in experience, her solutions to these questions and is also prepared to vary her methods according to her observation of the learning characteristics of individual children. Whether using i.t.a. or t.o. the teacher has to arrive at her own solutions about methods. It may well be that i.t.a. simplifies the problem and that the choice of methods can be more clearly made.

The word 'method' may also be used to refer to the way the teacher plans to take children through the sequence of stages and skills in learning to read. There is the stage of the first visual and auditory discriminations and meaning-symbol associations at the beginning; the stage of systematically developing word-recognition skills; the stage of acquiring phrase reading and fluency; the stage of independent reading with good comprehension for enjoyment and information. We have to ask which of these stages is most assisted by the use of i.t.a. (presumably the first two) and how far its effects spread over to the others.

The main benefit we would expect is that i.t.a. might accelerate the learning of word-recognition skills: i.e. what Downing refers to as 'lower order decoding skills'. The reported results suggest that this is so. Children (at least many of them and most noticeably the brighter) proceed more quickly through their basic reading books and are significantly more advanced than children learning in t.o. after $1\frac{1}{2}$ years (Table E2). In the third year this remains true, though the t.o. group appear to have made ground when both groups are tested in t.o. Since accuracy and speed of reading are both related to word-recognition skill, we would expect a comparable superiority of the i.t.a. group on these measures and this also is found to be the case. But it has to be noted that the difficulties which slow down the t.o. group in the early stages affect the i.t.a. group to some extent at the transition stage and the difference between the mean word-recognition ages in the seventh term is only 5 months of Reading Age (Table E 22). (It is a pity that there are no results on a word-recognition test at the end of the third year.)

The results of testing reading comprehension are not so clear. The Neale comprehension scores favour the i.t.a. group but the Standish test shows no significant difference. One would not, however, predict so confidently that a regularized spelling should result in better comprehension. In so far as i.t.a. facilitates the development of fluent accurate reading, it would be expected to benefit comprehension. In so far as it makes possible a wider experience of reading stories and information books at a somewhat earlier point in time, it would be expected to benefit comprehension in some measure. But good reading with comprehension depends on much more beside 'lower order decoding skills' and fluency. It depends on children's maturity of experience, their range of concepts, the quality and range of their vocabulary, and their general linguistic maturity as well as the emphasis given to it in teaching. In brief, in evaluating i.t.a. research we should not expect too great benefits from it in aspects of the reading process where its effects are indirect. Likewise, in considering whether to use i.t.a. in practice there could be a danger of expecting too much from it. It is unlikely to be a panacea for reading problems. Its main contribution is likely to be in one part of the process of learning to read; its contribution to other parts and other problems seems to me to need further evaluation.

That i.t.a. accelerates the process of learning to read in the early stages is a strong point in its favour. Even though final achievements may not be markedly or conclusively superior, there may well be less tangible benefits such as feelings of success, the development of learning sets in reading and greater freedom in written work (though I think that teachers' attitudes to written work are very influential). But a more potent argument for i.t.a. would be available if it could be shown that its use resulted in fewer failures in reading. To my mind, this would be a more solid benefit than an acceleration of progress in reading in the majority of children who are already successfully taught. From the tables and charts available, it is difficult to be certain on this point. There are certainly more children (Table E1) still on Book 1 or 2 after $2\frac{1}{2}$ years in the t.o. group than the i.t.a. but there are still 15 per cent. of the experimental group still at this stage. It looks as though some still lag behind although others speed ahead.

Children who fail in reading are, of course, of many kinds. Some fail as a result of a combination of unfavourable personal and environmental factors. i.t.a. might be expected to benefit these only in so far as its regularity reduces the difficulty of the learning

Evaluations

task. Others, one feels, have failed to learn because they lack 'readiness' (and sometimes the appropriate teaching) for the next stage of the process of learning to read. Some, for example, are not ready to make the auditory discriminations and generalizations in phonic work; and sometimes phonic teaching fails to take account of differences in phonic readiness. It would appear likely that i.t.a. would help such children. Downing notes that 'i.t.a. pupils appear to show readiness for phonics somewhat earlier than is usual when t.o. is used'. A useful point for evaluating i.t.a. would be information about whether its use minimizes the difficulties of such children, who are common among backward readers in t.o. and who show confusions and gaps in their knowledge of phonics. A comparison of the diagnostic pattern of reading difficulties in children brought up on i.t.a. and t.o. as well as a comparison of the proportion of failures on both would be valuable. I would expect such a comparison to favour i.t.a., but I would nevertheless expect a proportion of i.t.a. children to show some of the common difficulties we meet in backward readers, since the source of some of the difficulties are in the pupils themselves and not simply in traditional orthography.

I suggested earlier that we should not expect i.t.a. to do what, by the nature of the process of learning to read, it could not be expected to do. Results from the slow learners are a case in point. Most schools have a few children who are mentally and personally immature. They are often linguistically retarded; their perceptual development is not up to the tasks of visual and auditory discrimination; and their visual-motor performance is poor, as shown in immature drawings and shape-copying. We would not expect them to make quick progress in the infant school. Indeed they need a preparation for reading with a view to more definite instruction later in the infant school. (It would be interesting to know whether the 17 per cent. of i.t.a. pupils still on or below Book 2 after 2 years are entirely such children, or whether this percentage includes children with other kinds of difficulty.) But, as Downing rightly points out, teaching reading to slow learners needs to extend into the junior school. In present circumstances with t.o. these children, cannot always be assured on a continuation of infant methods in the first year or so in the junior school and this is one of the problems aggravating the problem of backwardness. It is pertinent to raise the question of what will happen to children who make a start on i.t.a. in the infant school and do not transfer to t.o. before going to the junior department. In considering the use of i.t.a., steps will have to be taken to ensure that i.t.a. can be efficiently continued, otherwise it will bear hard on slow learners and reading failures whose need for improved methods of instruction is the greatest.

Another question in relation to slow learners is the length of time they spend on i.t.a. If they are exposed to i.t.a. in the infant school and need to continue into the junior school, some of them are going to be reading i.t.a. for a very much longer time than average and bright children. The same question will arise with educationally subnormal children whose progress through the early stages of reading is spread out over a much longer period of time. Will there be any adverse effects? For example, will the temporary regression after transfer to t.o. be more marked with them? Another practical question is—how long, in fact, should the slowest children remain on i.t.a.? Among very backward children in ordinary and special schools are some who, for a combination of reasons, have made little progress. The answer may be that with i.t.a. this would not happen but one feels that there *are* children whose difficulties are other than the difficulties of t.o. What should be the recommendation in their case? Should they transfer to t.o. even though they are not ready? Presumably the further research on i.t.a. with slow learners will provide some answers.

Of all the factors influencing progress in reading in schools, I believe the most important is the teacher's understanding of the processes involved in learning to read—and how, on this basis, to organize instruction in large heterogeneous classes. In particular, the role of the headteacher is crucial in developing a system of reading instruction and getting it put into effect by a combination of guidance, demonstration and participation. For a complete evaluation of i.t.a. one would like to know from teachers how it has affected their teaching in practice—at what points procedures normal in teaching with t.o. have been omitted or reduced, introduced earlier or in different ways. For example, one of the problems in teaching reading is organizing within the same class for a wide spread of attainment. The need is shown rather clearly in Table E 1, with a quarter of the t.o. children still on Book 1 or 2 after $2\frac{1}{2}$ years. An advantage of i.t.a. may be that more children proceed quickly to independence in reading leaving fewer children requiring individual or group help. On the other hand, are there problems in organizing for transfer in a part of the class while the remainder are still on i.t.a.? To consider another question: one of the problems in the early stages of teaching reading is the planning of systematic phonic work, and particularly the timing of it and its relationship to the total reading programme. Presumably, these problems are simplified in i.t.a. at

Evaluations

this stage and some of them may occur in some degree at the stage of transfer. It would be useful to have the impressions of teachers on these and other practical questions since so much has been written by those who have not actually done the teaching.

It may well be that i.t.a. makes it easier to organize a coherent programme of reading instruction in a school. If this were thought to be so, I think we should, however, need to distinguish between what might happen were i.t.a. in general use, and no longer a novelty, from what happens when a few schools take it up and are no doubt provoked by the new medium into thinking about and discussing the teaching of reading. (The possibility that this occurred to some extent in the experimental schools in the first i.t.a. experiment is a small factor which should be considered in evaluation, as well as the Hawthorne Effect.)

The results of the first i.t.a. experiment provide some positive evidence in favour of i.t.a., and to this I would be inclined to add the favourable impression of teachers who have used the medium. As the initial shortage of experimental schools shows, teachers are slow to hazard the unusual—but, having tried, judge by results. (How many of the experimental schools are continuing with i.t.a.?) There do appear to me to be several aspects of the use of i.t.a. on which we could do with further information, viz. its use with slow learners, and its effects on the incidence of intelligent children who fail in reading; and we also need information from teachers themselves about its use and the contribution it makes to the organization of reading instruction.

Evaluations—5

JAMES HEMMING
Educational Psychologist

IT would be wrong to regard the present controversy concerning the early stage of learning to read as 'i.t.a. versus the rest'. For one thing, more than i.t.a. as such is involved in the discussion that has developed around i.t.a.; on the other hand, wide variation exists in methods used other than i.t.a. One can find schools where the children themselves make their first reading books; schools that concentrate work around a course of infant readers; schools that minimize the use of a course, depending for development of skill upon the mixed stimulus provided by a graded class library; schools including more or less phonic practice, and so on. The situation is, in fact, more complex than the simple challenge of a unified standard method by a revolutionary new approach. I think, then, we should take a look at the current theoretical position of infant reading before considering the research findings on i.t.a.

Since the establishment of the characteristic method of teaching reading in our infant classes—we might call it 'look-and-say-plus-phonics'—a great deal of new information has become available about linguistics, children's ability to deal with language, perception, infant logic, and how children learn. This means that we should need to re-think reading theory, at the present time, even if i.t.a. had not appeared. The new knowledge does not cast doubt upon look-and-say as one element in teaching reading, but it does refute some of the assumptions that the early Look-and-say theorists made and promulgated, and which still live on in theory and action. It is important, today, to dissociate look-and-say, as a useful technique and source of stimulus to the beginner, from the erroneous assumptions which have become an obstacle to the development of better methods for teaching children to read. To be more specific, let us examine four assumptions which have for some time been getting in the way of advance and consistency in reading theory:

(1) *That English is not a phonetic language and, therefore, children should be encouraged to develop other cues rather than phonic cues in recognizing words and differentiating one word from another.*

Evaluations

In fact, English *is* a phonetic language, built up of sound-units (phonemes), syllables, words, word groups, sentences, etc. Reading is made difficult for the young reader not because English is unphonetic but because it is rather disorderly phonetically, with single phonemes represented in different ways (e, ee, ea, ie, ei, y for example), single letters standing for more than one phoneme (c, y, s), and so on. Deliberately to develop other than phonic cues to word-recognition at the start of reading is both to deny the linguistic characteristics of English and to misuse the child's developing logical powers.

(2) *That young children lack the auditory discrimination to deal with the phonic structure of words.*

Here again the evidence is quite to the contrary. Children are born linguists. It looks as though the best time to learn a second language orally is before the age of ten. Children of ordinary ability born into bi-lingual communities learn to communicate freely in both languages simultaneously. African children, born into a community using a tonic language whose subtleties defeat most adult Europeans, acquire their mother tongue without difficulty; European children who are brought up in close contact with such a language also acquire it effortlessly, along with English. Faced with these realities of the powers of young children, we can forget about any supposed obligation to defend them from the phonic elements of language. We should, rather, surround them with consistent cues that they can pick up the moment they are ready to do so.

(3) *That children perceive wholes more easily than they perceive the elements of wholes; therefore the discrimination of individual letters should be avoided at the start of reading.*

Once again, the assumption goes beyond the evidence. It is true that we tend to organize our perceptions into wholes (gestalt theory), but the configuration of a letter is a whole in its own right, just as much as a word is. The inadequacy of this assumption is obvious the moment we turn from teaching reading to teaching number. Nobody, I think, would deny that children need to know the configuration of each numeral in a compound number in order to deal intelligently with such a number. In fact, good perception is not a matter of wholes *or* parts; synthesis and analysis proceed together. In this lies the effectiveness of structural apparatus in early number work: children learn the composition and decomposition of numbers at the same time.

The i.t.a. Symposium

(4) *That swift readers deal with words and sentences at a glance; therefore we should avoid drawing attention to letters as symbols if we want children to become swift readers.*

This assumption ignores the stages by which the capacity for rapid, well-adapted response to stimuli is developed in the brain. We still have a lot to learn about this, of course, but what seems to happen is that elements of experience gradually become elaborated into complex schemata which permit rapid, appropriate, co-ordinated response to a whole range of stimuli. The split-second decision of a good games player is an example of this. Such skilled response does *not* arise from studying wholes in isolation from their elements but from elaborating a number of components into co-ordinated systems of rapid reaction. A good reader is a good reader because he has acquired an efficient total response to the reading task, *based on a thorough grasp of its elements.*

These changes in our assumptions mean that we should now give up our former shyness about introducing letter-consciousness and phonics in early reading. This is not to move backwards towards the tedious illogicalities of alphabetic and phonic 'systems' of learning to read, but forward to a new synthesis in developing reading skill—one which helps children to understand the logic of their phonetic language from the start of learning to read, along with all the excitement and pleasure of reading and writing language which is full of meaning for them. This, let it be noted, is to go beyond the 'global' method, which often boils down to look-and-say supplemented by a barely related phonic practice sector. Phonic cues should be built in *through what is read.* The child needs the experience of the discovery and reinforcement that come from the successful application, in reading attack, of phonic cues as he acquires them.

The modification of method which the evidence strongly suggests we must undertake can be met in one of two ways. We can so combine look-and-say with phonic insight in what we offer for reading that the logic of the language is made available to the child in spite of our disorganized orthography, or we can regularize the orthography so that the phonic logic of our language is immediately obvious—the i.t.a. solution. Either solution gives us what we need, the *dual* reinforcement of reading skill arising from whole-word recognition, and word-attack through phonic understanding, going along side by side and mutually supporting each other. Which solution is the better? Unfortunately we still cannot say because, as yet, no research series has been carried out and evaluated, so far

Evaluations

as I am aware, in which i.t.a. classes have been matched with classes using a t.o. course designed on the principles I have outlined. Meanwhile, Downing's i.t.a. research, reported in this publication, gives us some indication of what happens when a logic of understanding is made available to children learning to read.

I would now like to consider i.t.a. as a solution to our infant reading problem under two heads: a brief comment on the research as such, and an assessment of i.t.a. as a method of introducing children to reading. There are, inevitably, criticisms that can be directed at the methodology of the research. My chief one would be that one cannot really use, for purposes of comparing attainment between t.o. and i.t.a. groups of children, tests that were standardized in their t.o. form, and have been translated into i.t.a. for the purpose of the research. This applies particularly to Schonell's Graded Word Reading Test. The list of words in this test gradually becomes more difficult to read, partly because of spelling difficulties, partly because of increasing length, and partly because of increasing unfamiliarity. Once translated into i.t.a., the first of these three variables is eliminated. Thus, in i.t.a., the word *ceiling* (the 33rd. in the list) becomes no more difficult to read than *little* (the 2nd word in the list).

Nevertheless, it seems to me that Downing establishes his case that children learn to read more quickly and efficiently with i.t.a. Nor am I much impressed by those critics who put this down to Hawthorne Effect. If Hawthorne Effect is indeed as great as some critics suggest, then we should have to write off here and now all research into method based on matched groups hitherto attempted, including much of the research on which the methods supported by the critics are based. In passing, however, I should say that Downing's method of attempting to neutralize Hawthorne Effect seems to me a good deal less effective than would be obtained from a longitudinal study of matched groups in the same school and under the same teacher, year after year, to see how much, if at all, learning falls off as i.t.a. itself loses its freshness of impact.

Early improvement accepted, we are still left with three questions. (1) Do the bright pupils suffer because they cannot apply i.t.a. to reading outside the classroom? (2) Is the check occurring on transfer to t.o. too high a price to pay for greater facility at the start? (3) How far is the whole situation at risk because i.t.a. requires teachers who believe in the new method and are ready to learn it? I would like to make some comments on all three questions.

The i.t.a. Symposium

The discrepancy, when i.t.a. is used, between classroom reading and the environmental stimulus to read, is no more, I would have thought, than the discrepancy that already exists, insofar as small letters are usually taught before capital letters, whereas most environmental words likely to obtrude on the child's attention—street names, car number plates, shop signs, traffic signs, etc.—are in capital letters. However, the discrepancy could be frustrating if an able child was held back from transfer to t.o. beyond the point when he was ready for it.

To turn to the second question, *some* check at transfer is a small price to pay for heightened confidence in the early stages. The research report suggests that the check is not serious. Nevertheless, research directed to discovering the level of confidence, and pleasure in reading, in both t.o. and i.t.a. groups, before and after transition, would be welcome. This could be done by precisely matching Book Corner and other play facilities and then recording how many pupil-minutes were voluntarily spent in Book Corners during a sample of free activity periods. What seems to me to be vital is that teaching shall be so individualized that transfer to t.o. is on a personal, not on a group basis. This would be to follow normal infant method, but the temptation would be there, all the same, to handle the transition in over-large ability groupings.

Question three—teacher response—is plainly of immense importance. Whereas Hawthorne Effect probably does not count for much in infant classrooms, teacher morale most certainly does. Teachers who are forced into i.t.a. against their wishes would be likely to suffer a decline in confidence and enthusiasm which would affect their competence as teachers.

The point here is that a school should not go over to i.t.a. by a decision made independently of the wishes of the teachers. If discussions on i.t.a. with the staff did not indicate an interest in making the experiment, then the introduction of i.t.a. would be likely to arouse a resentment that would more than offset the methodological advantage of i.t.a. In the last analysis, the best method for any infant teacher to use is the one in which she believes. Which is not to say that innovation should not be encouraged.

Evaluation—6

JACK A. HOLMES
University of California, Berkeley

FIRST, it must be stressed that Downing made a distinct point of *not* claiming that he was able to control all the 'incidental' variables in his experiment. Nevertheless, to this reviewer, it is apparent that he made a concerted effort to reduce to a minimum any bias that could have arisen from such 'nuisance' variables.

Initially, this reduction of bias was done by attempting to match the Experimental Groups (i.t.a.) with the Control Groups (t.o.) on intelligence, age, sex, social class, size of school, pupil-teacher ratio, urban/rural location, type of school organization, and certain school amenities. Furthermore, beyond the matching, the experimental design called for an attempt to create an *artificial* Hawthorne Effect in the Control Groups to balance that which seemed likely to arise in the Experimental Groups. Finally, while Downing was not able to get teachers to volunteer to teach either i.t.a. or t.o. as might be dictated by a random assignment of teachers to treatments, he at least attempted to match them on the basis of preference for i.t.a. or t.o.

Despite Downing's exhaustive effort to reduce possible bias by matching, the technique carries with it some inherent difficulties. As expected, the rigorous attempt to adhere to broad-scale matching materially reduced the size of his sample; and, therefore, all his data could not be utilized. Such a loss is of grave concern, first, because ordinarily the consequence is ruinous to a longitudinal study and, second, because a certain bias may be introduced by discarding groups for which a match cannot be found.

Unless one has engaged in a large-scale longitudinal experiment, one cannot really appreciate the many major and minor problems that arise to threaten and often actually disrupt the most carefully planned experimental designs. This is especially true where interests, prerogatives of control, and traditional procedures come into conflict with the good experimental design. Publishers, administrators, supervisors, teachers, and parents alike jealously guard their traditional domains of control to such an extent that the 'elegant' research design always seems to come off second best in a field study—and Downing's study was no exception. Rigidity on the part of administrators did, in fact, raise havoc with the normal randomization process in this study.

It would be a relatively simple matter to set an ideal but unrealistically high *post hoc* standard for the experiment, and from such a position just as unrealistically proceed to cut the study to ribbons. However, this reviewer prefers to temper the tone of his critical remarks by his considered judgment of the difficulties Downing faced.

On this basis then, this reviewer is impressed with the tenacity with which Downing strove for objectivity throughout all phases of his study. He exhibited ingenuity in contriving and carrying out, over a three-year period, a design which seems to have utilized the best in his data. *His step-by-step analysis is thorough and cautious and his concluding remarks are conservative. Further, his discussion of the weakness in i.t.a. brought to light by the study, definitely points to a new hope on the horizon.* In short, the study is an exceptional piece of work even though certain limitations markedly reduce the extent to which one can generalize its findings.

Perhaps it is wise to point out some of the weaknesses and specific limitations in this study, in order to decide to what extent one may accept the results. One cannot quarrel with Downing's meticulous matching of schools (classes), but unfortunately, after matching, he was not able to randomly assign from each matched pair one class to his Experimental Group and the other to his Control Group. Nor was he able to randomly allocate his teachers to the Experimental and Control classes. To appraciate the significance of these limitations it should be understood that what is accomplished by matching is not the same as that which is accomplished by randomization. One matches to equate groups, but one randomizes the assignment of treatments to the member pairs of the matched groups so that the results may be generalized from the working sample to the target population. Fortunately, Downing was able to introduce a degree of randomization, but at best it was a hedged expedient. Of course, Downing himself recognized this shortcoming and initiated the 'Second British Experiment on i.t.a.'

Besides the lack of random assignment of Experimental and Control conditions and teachers to matched-paired classes, there was also a certain lack of control over the *method* (Look and say, Phonic, etc.) used in the i.t.a. and t.o. classes. A further complication arose when matching, and subsequent computation was done sometimes on the basis of schools, sometimes on the basis of classes, and sometimes on the basis of individuals. In the eyes of some authorities, this procedure would not be justified because they would say that the class is the only true teaching unit. However, it can be argued that the child is the true unit for learning. Both may be true, therefore, there may be some strength in Downing's procedure to 'look at the data from many angles'.

The choice of the Kolmogorov-Smirnov technique as his test statistic, though certainly acceptable, leaves something to be desired. However, Downing's greatest technical oversight in reporting the results was in *not* setting the alpha level at .05 *or* .01 *before* the experiment began and then sticking to it. This practice of switching back and forth from .05 to .01 in confidence levels as suited his purpose was not only technically inadvisable, but reflected a variable decision rule. Furthermore, there seemed to be a bit-by-bit application of the Kolmogorov-Smirnov test to each hypothesis, so that sight of an estimate of the experimental error was completely lost. One cannot but wonder what the overall experimental error might be, when over a hundred separate significance tests were reported.

However, it must be recognized, in Downing's defence, that the multiplication of hypotheses was unavoidable when he *had* to ask the same questions a number of times in order to measure term to term improvements in a longitudinal study. The assessment of increments of growth *within* and *between* the Experimental and Control Groups from term to term becomes increasingly messy when one's sample(s) are neither independent nor completely the same. This uncertainty is introduced in a longitudinal study when the experimenter must re-select by matching his units every term because of the uneven attribution in his successive samples. The selection of each successive sub-group always means a retesting of the 'Goodness' of the Experimental Control pairings on the many matching variables. This leaves something of a cloud over the results because one can never be absolutely sure of how the missing students, classes, or schools would have performed, had they stayed in the study. But this is one of the inherent and unavoidable hazards of any longitudinal study and must be expected as a reality with which to be dealt. Downing coped with it in the best way he could.

Because his sample had to be reconstituted from term to term from the shrinking original sample, Downing had to be a very good 'housekeeper' in order to keep so many separate comparisons straight. It was because of this marked increase in the number of hypotheses to be tested, with its corresponding drop in control of the experimental error, that one wishes he could have used a technique not unlike Scheffé's *post hoc* method of multiple contrasts. In this way he would have been able to keep the experimental error as well as the separate hypothesis error at a specified level.

Conclusions

Above, this reviewer has detailed the major criticisms as he sees them, and now would like to take a judicious look at the results of the study.

In spite of the limitations of the design and analyses (which, I am sure, Downing appreciates better than anyone else) each of the findings seems reasonable; and what is more, the credulity of each seems to be reinforced because they tend to 'hang together', to have an internal consistency, as it were.

Little purpose would be served by systematically reviewing each and all of the study's hypotheses, for the impact of the total study is clear: i.t.a., as it stands, definitely appears to have something to offer the field of reading. In a modified form, i.t.a. may become an extremely powerful tool for the teaching of reading. Without a doubt, Downing's i.t.a. Groups made greater reading gains than his t.o. Groups in their respective alphabets, and this was true whether improvement was assessed on the basic reader series or on lower-order decoding skills. Further, even when tested in t.o., the Experimental Groups did better than the Control Groups in reading accuracy and comprehension at the end of the *third* school year. Likewise, the Experimental Group pupils used more words in their themes than did the Control Group pupils. However, this last statement must be tentative because, as Downing says, the assignment of the theme topics was not controlled.

The two surprise findings for this reviewer were: (a) that the higher the level of the achiever, the more he was assisted by i.t.a. in learning to read and to spell in t.o., and (b) that the Hawthorne Effect failed to mateialize in the Control Groups. Therefore, Downing suggested that the importance of the so-called Hawthorne Effect in educational experiments may be exaggerated. If so, this finding invites further research.

Downing correctly put his finger on the problem of 'transfer', as the heart of any technique that would start children on the road to reading through a modified orthography.

Although i.t.a. pupils were superior to t.o. pupils on the basic measures of reading achievement, they were not as good as they might have been had they been allowed to continue in i.t.a. That is, significant slippage from i.t.a. to t.o. was observed, and it was apparently due to problems in transfer. Downing wisely points out that transfer could be facilitated if the teaching materials, methods, and the timing of the transition stage from i.t.a. to t.o. were better understood so that the teacher would know how to maximize the chances of transfer in her students.

Downing points to Burt's early statement that, after all, i.t.a. was constructed as a special case with little reference to previous research and teachers' experiences.

In summary, this reviewer heartily agrees with Downing's call for a series of experiments in the 'psychological laboratory' designed to determine how the forms of i.t.a. characters ought to be modified to maximize their transfer value to t.o.; and further to find what new materials and teaching techniques should be developed to facilitate transfer from i.t.a. to t.o. For it appears, that Downing was well within the limitations of his study when he said, 'The unequivocal conclusion from the results of these experiments is that the traditional orthography of English is an important cause of difficulty in teaching and learning reading and writing in English-speaking countries.'

All in all, 'The First British Experiment with i.t.a.' is clearly conceived, well controlled, and thoroughly objective in its design. As a field study it met a number of disturbing difficulties—all of which were overcome, albeit with some loss in the elegance of the design and restriction of the generalizability of the finding. In this reviewer's judgment it is a worthy study. Downing is to be congratulated for 'pulling it off' in spite of the inherent difficulties in a longitudinal study, and in spite of resistance on the part of teachers and administrators to try such a radical procedure as i.t.a.

Evaluations—7

A. R. MacKinnon
Simon Fraser University, Burnaby, B.C.

THIS report represents another facet of a large social experiment in the introduction of orthographic modifications in the teaching of English. Unlike other efforts aimed at reform of English spelling, this experiment had its locus almost immediately in many schools and sought *not* to replace traditional orthography but to encourage instead an *easier transition* to the written language of the culture.

The introduction to the report makes clear that the experiment was concerned with the introduction of a 'transitional writing system' which would not change in any radical way the teaching procedures already extant or the major objectives of instruction. Instead, the innovation was to be concerned with improving the efficiency of something which was taking place already. Since any attempt to modify or alter the language of a culture can quickly prompt disruptive emotions, such a compromise approach tended to diminish resistance, aroused the enthusiasm of some spelling reformers and permitted the experiment to begin and to flourish.

It has been a courageous social experiment to date which has challenged the 'establishment' at every level from senior government bureaux and large publishing houses through to the ultra-conservatism of many classroom teachers. The social context of the experiment has engendered sharp debate and argument not only in the United Kingdom but also throughout North America and the rest of the English-speaking world. Right from the outset of the experiment through to the present day, the study has been conducted on a molar, global scale. It is not unexpected, accordingly, that there are no negative findings on i.t.a. reported.

The hypotheses raised have been confirmed for all the questions (with some minor qualifications in certain cases). Such a situation tends to be typical of an ongoing social experiment aimed at producing innovation. What would happen if all the hypotheses had been rejected is difficult to imagine given the present social context of the experiment! The elaborate 'controls' placed on the study almost immediately guaranteed the outcomes since it was impossible for any significant disruptive factors to impinge on the programme. Thus, volunteers for both 'control' and 'experimental' groups had to

Evaluations

commit themselves for the duration of the study in spite of the fact that certain early gains would soon indicate the winning 'side'. Carefully constructed information papers were developed supporting i.t.a. and were widely disseminated which certainly touched off long-felt uneasiness about traditional orthography. Any extensive evaluation was delayed until sufficient time had elapsed to establish some positive aspects of the innovation. Downing points out (page 5) that research design and choice of instruments was governed by a 'general principle that the evaluation *should be immediately meaningful to teachers and administrators*'. This certainly suggests that i.t.a. could be of use and value and should be employed. All these procedures (and many more) have the characteristics of a well-constructed social experiment for introducing change. The total global enterprise deserves commendation for its intensive efforts and its meteoric success in the introduction of the innovation.

There is little to be gained, however, in the research report from what is already current information. The quasi-scientific documentation falls into a trap all too common in educational research. Once a programme is launched, attempts are made to establish through very questionable comparison procedures what was largely expected from the outset. It is simply impossible to control all the variables that are involved in such a social experiment. Further, there are no evaluation procedures available which can isolate all the critical dimensions of learning which should be involved in reading. This is not to say that Downing omitted any of the accepted practice in design—the procedures are most elaborate—but that such a study obscures many questions simply by its massiveness and tends to suggest conclusions which could be quite misleading. Thus, it would be singularly unwise to assume that i.t.a. had been *proven* as *the* effective teaching medium for first steps in learning to read. The report makes no such claim and we are left still with the problems of simplification and the difficulties of traditional orthography.

What does emerge is the need for the intensive study of children's learning in juxtaposition with various kinds of simplification designs. The response to i.t.a. on the part of teachers and learners indicates that something *can* be done which will reduce unnecessary difficulties. Far from worrying about the Hawthorne Effect in the study, the phenomenon should have been welcomed as part of the stimulation needed to raise up insistent questions which have lain dormant too long.

The i.t.a. Symposium

The comparisons which have been made (with their strong support for i.t.a.) will now assure that the social experiment will continue. This should give the context for intensive small-scale investigations which can illumine the problem of learning more specifically. It would seem unwise to replicate the study undertaken in the United Kingdom for the simple reason that it would be impossible. It would be more relevant to design those investigations which can be replicated and to aim at molecular inquiry rather than a massive, statistical study. Above all, the studies should *not* be initiated, planned, managed and evaluated by just one agency.

There is urgent need to perceive through investigations precisely *what* a child *does* when he learns to read. Children are surrounded by a print medium culture of traditional orthography long before they arrive at school. It could well be that a child must make an adjustment to the new orthography used by the school as contrasted with that which he may be able to recognize in his out-of-school environment. If this is so there would be, first, a transition to i.t.a. and, secondly, a transition to the traditional orthography employed by the school. In fact there could well be a number of transitions needed for children throughout their years at school.

In the current research report there is great difficulty in isolating what difficulties were caused by the design of instructional material and those prompted by i.t.a. or t.o. It is widely recognized that the current design promotes a great deal of unnecessary difficulty which is not only due to the orthography employed. Studies in psycholinguistics particularly have shown that difficulties arise at the perceptual, phonemic, semantic and syntactic levels either all together or in various combinations. Active steps are now being taken by linguists to design materials which will more clearly show the correspondence existing between speech and its written notations and how far that correspondence goes. Other research workers are engaged in the complex task of building and testing materials which will unite cognitive processes simultaneously into an organic structure for growth. It could well be that much of the simplification theory inherent now in i.t.a. could be incorporated in these developments.

Attention will focus undoubtedly in future studies on the analysis of errors to attain insight on mental processes and where they go astray. The section in the report dealing with spelling errors is more in this research direction. Comparisons with i.t.a. and other orthographies within a proper learning sequence could yield rich data on children's cognitive operations. Also, analysis of creative

Evaluations

writing could yield cues to more adequate design for promoting these generative processes *in writing* which a child has managed consummately well before school when he enters a command of spoken language.

There is good reason to look forward to Downing's forthcoming *Evaluating* i.t.a.: *1960-66,* since it could bring out some of the important considerations needed for evaluating reading growth. In the research report emphasis was placed on measurable gains primarily in terms of scores attained. Future evaluation will have to be concerned as much with how scores are arrived at as with the scores themselves. Unless this is done, much of the new design could result in encouraging the doing of something which should never have been attempted in the first place. Downing appears to be well aware of this, but the problem still remains of how to assess the type of growing comprehension essential in reading which is more clearly intelligence itself.

There is just one major danger in the i.t.a. social experiment and that is that the experiment will cease and a crusade will begin. There are signs already of many individuals with a messianic zeal for the materials. If the current report was seen as a passport for any wholesale acceptance, the numerous studies of simplification now under way would be greatly inhibited and countless children would suffer.

Evaluations—8

A. H. Morgan and M. Procter
School Psychological Service, Inner London Education Authority

COMMENT on Downing's paper must begin with recognition of the size and complexity of the task which, in 1960, he undertook and of the energy and ingenuity with which he has since been engaged on it. The planning of the inquiry, the recruitment and training of teachers, the stimulation of a flow of written material for schools, the testing assessment procedures have involved a full-time team at the Reading Research Unit. It was supported by numbers of 'seasonal' workers (testers) and probably several hundreds of teachers—the latter busily teaching and patiently recording, over a period of at least three years. One is also conscious that even so the resources available to the Unit could not have been adequate for a full investigation of each intriguing and important new field which would be temptingly revealed as the investigation progressed.

Criticism may therefore easily become 'unfair' in its reference to what are felt to be omissions. The fact that other, earlier, interim reports are available in which results so far are recorded and interpreted, albeit 'with caution', may also lead one to misrepresent unwittingly the present position.

The remarks which follow have arisen from our attempt to clarify the significance of the present report for advisers and teachers rather than for researchers.

This report does not deal with all available research on i.t.a. Important work is going on in America and no doubt elsewhere; it does not cover any work being carried out in Britain outside the responsibility of the Reading Research Unit; it does not cover all the work on i.t.a. in which the Unit is itself engaged. It deals only with the First Experiment—which, however, holds pride of place as the first, and major, exploration; and it is the most recent in a succession of reports on that. The first of this series of interim reports appeared in a paper presented in New York in November 1962. Others followed, apparently 'as part of the history of our work to date', and another fuller version is to succeed the present one. Even this may not be the definitive report, for it now appears that the final data may cover a three or four year cycle for each of the September Infant School intakes in the years 1961, 1962 and 1963—and this

Evaluations

may not yet have been gathered and analysed. The impression is left that it is a definitive report so far as the early stages of reading in i.t.a. are concerned: it is 'interim' so far as the transfer to t.o. in reading and writing is concerned.

Interim reports clearly have value for the experimenters; as a stock-taking, in which they may assure themselves that the experiment as planned is flowing smoothly in practice, or from which they may detect, and perhaps adjust to, unexpected and interesting developments. But if they are intended also for wider reading, each interim report would be more easily followed if it were explicitly related to the preceding one and perhaps to the following one. The present paper offers its record in relative isolation from its predecessors. This entails a prodigal amount of repetition of material and comment. It also demands a very careful reading, for as one progresses through the series of reports the data on which conclusions are based is changed: the method of analysis of the results is varied; and the conclusions themselves are modified, sometimes in substance and sometimes in the implications suggested by the emphasis, context or form of phrase. This is, of course, a natural response in an observer who is sensitive to the changes which may be revealed as the data is progressively acquired and scrutinized. There are some scattered references to this process in the report being considered. However, a most important corollary to the principle of statistically documented interim reports does seem to us to be the need to integrate present with past—and, if possible, future—reports in a quite explicit way. The current report should stand as an independent statement, important in its own right, but noting the developments and modifications which have occurred.

The aims of the experiment and their significance for teachers, as now given, appear to have changed in the emphasis given to the components. This, if the opinion is well founded, could again be a well-justified growth, whatever its difficulty for the readers. But it would benefit by being made explicit and supported by reasons. The University of London Institute of Education, in the pamphlet it published in June 1960 ushering in the inquiry, stated that despite the importance, and difficulty, of learning to read 'a variation in the roman alphabet itself, by augmentations specially designed for the early teaching of reading, has never yet been investigated in a scientific fashion'. The inquiry was to test the validity of the claims made by supporters and opponents of the augmented alphabet. 'The alphabet to be used will itself be on trial, and may as a

The i.t.a. Symposium

result, be modified.' 'Press, Television and Sound Broadcast support is being sought to enable the announcement of the launching of the research to gain . . . a nation-wide understanding and acceptance of the project so that, once it has begun the teachers and parents . . . may concentrate on their tasks free from disturbance.' Burt, in his introduction to tω bεε *or not to be* (Cassell), which was published in 1962, widened the conception of the aims, pointing out that not only might modifications of the Augmented Roman Alphabet (as it was then called) need to be considered, but also alternative types of rational orthography. In the same book (p.3) the aim was summarized as 'investigating the effectiveness of the Augmented Roman Alphabet as a medium for teaching reading' and this it seems is how it remained in most people's minds.

The present report seems now to rephrase and elaborate this aim in the following terms: (1) to investigate traditional orthography as a cause of difficulty in learning to read, using i.t.a. as a medium for the investigation (i.e. as one, not necessarily the best, alternative to t.o.); (2) if t.o. should be shown to be a major obstacle, to inquire into the nature of the difficulties it creates; and what could be done about them—should they be 'taught' better, or circumvented by a planned grading of their difficulty; should a complete transfer bemade to a simplified spelling (of a kind yet to be agreed) or would a transitional writing form be adequate? (3) In the latter case the question now becomes: what difficulties did i.t.a. as a writing system create, either in initial learning or on transfer to t.o. and can they be reduced, or is some different transitional writing system likely to be more suitable?

This change of formulation, if it is admitted as such, may make it more acceptable. It does, however, change the attitude with which one approaches the i.t.a. report. The question now is not a matter of 'to be or not to be?' i.e. shall we or shall we not, use i.t.a.? It is a broader set of questions which would have a relevance to reading whether i.t.a. were used or not. Yet it is on i.t.a. itself that the research so far has focussed, and evidence on these wider issues has been secondary.

This change in direction, or at least in emphasis, if valid, would be interesting to trace. One factor may have been implicit in the selected experimental design itself. The initial preparation by 'Press, Television and Sound Broadcasting' may have helped to narrow the issue to the simple question 'i.t.a. or not i.t.a.?' The use of the large scale 'field experiment' design meant that many administrators, teachers and parents would need persuading that this was not only an investigatition into possible difficulties arising from

Evaluations

t.o. but that the 'alternative' i.t.a. was a positive one likely to lead to great gain (especially since the initial reception of i.t.a. was that it was 'a bizarre idea'). The evaluation programme was indeed devised to 'be immediately meaningful to teachers and administrators'. The researcher could, in these circumstances, find himself balancing, or alternating, between the role of impartial experimenter and that of persuader, advocate and teacher. The publication of promising interim reports, the establishment in 1962—barely a year after i.t.a.'s introduction to schools—of an independent i.t.a. Foundation devoted to furthering the spread of i.t.a., the freeing of i.t.a. school books from a limited distribution to open purchase by any school, all would bring to the foreground the 'i.t.a. *v.* t.o.' issue and help to establish i.t.a. in the field as the *de facto* successor to t.o. in the early stages of reading.

The research was outstanding in another important way—very relevant to a field research study, though certainly very difficult to explore and probably beyond the resources available. It was an experiment in educational innovation, a process very pertinent to the present situation with great innovations pending, or in progress, in school organization, curriculum and methods. Tantalizing glimpses of the process appear in the report. Recruitment of the groups was made by approaching Directors of Education personally —seven agreed to help, presumably by arranging for the Experimenter to address a meeting of teachers; and six of these provided subjects. Within the six authorities, i.t.a. seemed to have been regarded as 'a bizarre idea' so that by September 1961 only 20 schools were found prepared to introduce i.t.a. for beginning reading. It subsequently spread to some 1,800 schools. An account of the initial reactions of the various community, administrative and school units when presented with a major new educational idea —and the reasons for these and the subsequent changes—would have been a valuable, (but difficult and perhaps dangerous!) exercise in the psychology of innovation.

Reading through the present statement of the conclusions based on this first experiment so far and tracing their development through earlier interim reports, there appears now to be a restriction in their number, a greater caution in their formulation and a change in emphasis and sometimes in content.

1. The 'most important and most definite conclusion that can be drawn from the results of this research' is 'the unequivocal conclusion . . . that the traditional orthography of English is an important cause of difficulty in teaching and learning reading and

writing in English-speaking countries' (p. 51). These claims that reading skills, especially the lower order ones of word-recognition and accuracy, are more quickly built up in i.t.a. than in t.o. are based on cumulative studies of the September intake in three successive years. This advantage appears to be not so great as reported in the earliest reports, but is still considerable. The observations on writing seem to be based however on only a small sample of 54 children in their seventh term at school, in schools which were not adequately matched. Such evidence as they produced suggested that in i.t.a. the children wrote in greater quantity and in a vocabulary nearer in size to their spoken vocabulary than children using t.o.—this, if later confirmed, is no small gain in itself, but it leaves open the question of whether what they wrote was better in quality in any deeper sense, or whether they just wrote *more* of the same sort of material.

2. The transfer in reading from i.t.a. to t.o. In December 1963 (*The* i.t.a. *Reading Experiment*, University of London Institute of Education, Studies in Education, p.119) the conclusion from the data analysed up to that time was: 'if the results of similar tests of later entrants into the experimental and control samples confirm the above then we may conclude that pupils can effectively transfer their training in i.t.a. reading to reading in t.o.' In the present report however 'an important setback . . . at the stage of transition from i.t.a. to t.o.' (p 49) is recorded. (This seems to be especially noticeable in word-recognition skills and accuracy and the paper discusses ways in which the loss on transfer to t.o. may be reduced.)

3. i.t.a. 'generally produces superior results in t.o. reading and in spelling by the end of the third school year' (p.49). So far as spelling is concerned, however, the data reported (p.43) is derived from tests given in the middle of the third school year and in the middle of the fourth school year: only in the *second* test does the difference between the i.t.a. and t.o. children become significant, and then at the five per cent. level.

For reading, the newness of the conclusion lies in the word 'generally'. It is now shown that the results are most favourable in the highest achievers. 'The slower-learning children do begin to show some benefit at the end of the third year, but the poorest ten per cent. show negligible improvement in test results' (p.49). It may be that it is still too soon to judge the full effect of i.t.a. on these slower-learning children, but clearly they will still remain a teaching

Evaluations

problem for the Junior school, although it seems to us, the context for the teacher could be significantly different.

It is noticeable that some of the conclusions which were enumerated in the earlier reports, with varying degrees of confidence, are not here elaborated—e.g. that children using i.t.a. show improved self confidence, greater enthusiasm for books, improved *creative writing* (our italics), changed attitudes to school work, improved problem-solving ability. Re-reading the earlier reports now, it could perhaps be said that these were not 'conclusions' in the statistical sense, but only statements of more general probability or even only of possibility. Whilst at least some of these may still remain worthy of exploration, a feature of the present report is a restriction of speculation (stimulating as this is) and a closer adherence to possibilities for which evidence of a different kind is being produced.

The teacher who reads this report in order to decide whether or not to use i.t.a., will not find definitive answers to many of the questions he will wish to pose. It may be that the Research would not now see i.t.a. as its central problem: but the teacher in any case often takes decisions, in the making of which educational research, incomplete or complete, cannot be the sole arbiter. If the present report gives no straight 'yea' or 'nay', however, there are implications which could be very relevant to teachers. Experience has shown that some of these need re-emphasizing. It becomes clear that instruction in i.t.a. should precede its use: it is not generally satisfactory simply to 'pick it up as you go' (and this implies too that instruction should be available). And having once been 'instructed' the teacher needs to be aware of the possibility of the spontaneous variation which seems to take place as new ideas are 'adapted to suit local needs' or 'the needs of my class', or interpreted to fit into one's own educational practices and beliefs.

The report could also support a view which recommended the teacher to take a more limited view of the function of i.t.a. than appears to be current, and to be continually aware that in its use constant vigilance is desirable since a new medium may lead to new problems. It would seem a safe start, for example, to take i.t.a. as a new medium for facilitating the transmutation of visual symbols to their spoken equivalents—for facilitating word recognition and accuracy. But it will not do this by itself, and it will not create the preliminary conditions in which learning is possible or in which the child will want to learn. The teacher must intervene (not necessarily 'instruct') and the better his 'intervention' the more easily and rapidly learning will take place. Similarly, it will not, of itself, lead to a greater love of reading, to a greater understanding, to greater appreciation, or to a greater personal response. It may make these *possible* but the teacher will need to intervene, and other circumstances be favourable, for this to happen. Nor will the transfer in reading from i.t.a. to t.o. necessarily be a spontaneous affair: the teacher may need to take steps to bring it about (and some steps may be better than others). In like fashion, the child using i.t.a. will not necessarily *want* to communicate in writing; this wish has to be awakened and usually by the teacher. Subsequently the child may write more, and use a fuller share of his own vocabulary, but it will not therefore be richer and better in quality—in its structure and content. i.t.a. may help to make these possible, but the teacher must add something to make them *actual*. The same position could be taken with regard to the transfer in spelling to t.o. The i.t.a. may be taken as a tool which may make *possible* the easier acquisition of certain basic skills such as word-recognition, and along with this achievement, skills of a higher order may be built up leading to a general advance in a wider range of literary skills. But the tool can not be better than the workman who uses it; it can make some things *possible*, but it is the workman who must make them *actual*. The i.t.a. might, for example, lead to a rapid increase in the facility for 'barking at print' (used in its worst sense), though this need not be the fault of i.t.a. but of the way in which it was used by the teacher.

To some extent, a teacher who reasoned thus could be underestimating the contribution i.t.a. could make, but this could also be an error in the right direction. He would begin from the position that results are obtained not *by* i.t.a. but by a teacher working *with* i.t.a., in his own special way and special circumstances: i.t.a. is only the medium through which he must try to make other things come to pass. It may also remind him that, when all is done, the absolute differences in children's progress may remain as great as ever and that many influences, additional to the particular writing-form employed, affect the growth of communication skills, and provide him with a simultaneous challenge.

Evaluations—9

MARIE D. NEALE
Senior Lecturer in Education, The University of Sydney

THE primary impact of the report of i.t.a. on this writer is of excitement, admiration for the boldness of the British plan and intellectual curiosity concerning the implications of issues raised by the investigation. One feels a sense of urgency to capitalize upon the current findings in further innovation and experiment. Enthusiasm is somewhat tempered, however, by the realization that all research requires not only a happy alliance of academic, professional and personal talent, but considerable patience in the preparatory stages. It is sobering to consider that in the light of modern knowledge this imaginative attempt to document data in a subject that underpins every aspect of the educative process should have met with forces of prejudice, resistance and limited finance. Not that the report details or dwells upon these limiting factors. Rather do the latter emerge as an after-image as the reader pursues the train of reflections and questions set in motion by the findings of the research.

One is also uncomfortably aware that educational research is still a 'one man show' despite the backing of eminent scholars and the tendency in other sciences towards inter-disciplinary research projects. Again, while the findings are of utmost relevance to the life of a nation, one is struck by the manner in which the research writer has had to meet orthodox criteria in research methodology while exercising care in deferring to the opinions of head teachers, teachers and public. While one admires this English characteristic of respect for the rights of individuals to their personal interpretation of education, one cannot help considering that little progress would be made in other disciplines, e.g. in medicine, if clinical and scientific research waited upon the interests of the busy practitioner on the one hand, and the ambivalent attitudes of the public on the other. Thus this report on the studies of i.t.a. takes one to a consideration of issues far beyond the scope of its original theme, not least being the significance of the preparation of teachers-in-training for participation in research in such a way that they will maintain, during their professional career, an active intelligent interest in the trends of scientific inquiry. But perhaps, for the purposes of this brief introduction, it suffices to say that this British experiment represents an important milestone attained by educational research. Half a century of theory and research have culminated in a maturity that will now countenance a courageous original investigation of the teaching medium itself within the ongoing life of the schools. Whatever reservations one may have about specific aspects of the project, one must recognize that it has revealed the need for a critical re-appraisal of children's readiness for learning, the transfer of learning skills, the role of reading effectiveness in creativity, the significance of difficulties in early school learning upon the total development of children and the effect of research interest on the teacher's day-to-day practice in the schools.

With the volumes of research written in the field of reading, it is easy to assume that present teaching practices are founded on answers obtained to empirical inquiry. The fact that a large percentage of children learn to read within the first three years of school tends to reinforce this assumption, and to eradicate from memory the proportion of children who master only with painful slowness, the identification and recognition of symbols basic to the reading process. Nevertheless, abundant research literature testifies to the difficulties of many children in learning to read, together with numerous accounts of experimental methods employed to facilitate the development of perceptual skills. Many of the findings of these researches have also been compounded by the fact that anxiety is a frequent concomitant feature of failure to read. Intellectual inferiority, neurological dysfunction, emotional disturbances, poor motivation, and personality factors such as socio-cultural background, contribute to further confusion in relating research findings to educational practice. The investigation by Downing is refreshing in that it breaks new ground in three major ways:

I. The study is of intact samples of 'normal' young children, some only four years of age, learning to read within the natural setting of their local school. It is also a longitudinal investigation of the rate at which these children acquire related literacy skills.

II. The focus of the attention is upon the *medium* for teaching in contrast to the usual preoccupation of research with *methods* of teaching to read. The originality of the inquiry lies in a comparative study of the inhibiting or facilitating effects of teaching reading by means of either the traditional English orthography, or by the medium of a specially designed orthography. Sir James Pitman's Augmented Roman Alphabet has been devised to eliminate a number of the irregularities and inconsistencies of the grapheme-phoneme relationships of the English language to provide a simpler initial teaching alphabet, i.t.a.

III. The research plan incorporates a novel study of transfer in learning, as children taught with i.t.a. transfer their coding skills from the simpler linguistic system to the more complex traditional orthography.

Education of the Young Child

Looking at each of these aspects of the study in turn, the findings concerning the attainments of infant school children using i.t.a. leave no room for conjecture. The data indicate clearly that children using i.t.a. achieve a significant head-start in the mechanics of reading, or coding skills, when compared with their controls using traditional orthography. When one considers, for example, that in New South Wales new entrants to the infant schools are only gradually being inducted into the formal skills of reading after their first year, the achievements of the i.t.a. *first year* pupils are most impressive. Thus, after three terms of schooling 10.9 per cent. of the experimental children are reading Book 4 of their basic reader series as against 2.8 per cent. of the controls, while 5.7 per cent. of the experimental group are reading beyond Book 5 in contrast to none of the controls. What is even more striking to research worker and teacher alike, is the rapidity of progress beyond the first year, exemplified by 78.1 per cent. of i.t.a. children who pass through their fifth reader in the ensuing four terms, compared with 37.8 per cent. of the controls. If doubt exists concerning the validity of assessing progress by means of basic readers, this is eliminated by a study of the significantly higher scores obtained by the i.t.a. children on formal tests of graded work-recognition skills, and accuracy of reading in standardized prose passages. Nor can the criticism be levelled that the significant difference merely relates to 'barking at print', for, again in tests of reading-comprehension, there is unequivocal superiority of the experimental group.

These findings represent a revolutionary break-through in current psychological thinking, toppling one of the long established cornerstones in educational practice—that of 'readiness' for reading. Readiness has been a convenient hypothetical construct to subsume an extraordinary range of personality and learning variables which have to be appraised in establishing the appropriate 'teachable moment'. Teachers have been taught to delay the introduction of reading skills to infant children until they have a mental ability of six or seven years, a background of first hand experiences with the cultural aspects of their environment, ability to communicate impressions, observations and ideas, ability to comprehend instruction in a group situation, interest in pictures, and the meaning of written or printed symbols, social adjustment and the feeling of security, etc. (Gray, 1956, Sutton, 1955). The rationale for the delay in formal teaching is that children will acquire the perceptual skills more readily and with enhanced confidence when they reach an appropriate stage of maturity. On this latter point, however, there has been no clear unanimity, and there are well marked cultural differences in the age considered desirable for beginning the teaching of reading. Recently from quite disparate lines of research there have been findings which challenge the underlying assumptions of the readiness construct. These are in accord with the long unheeded observations, made by many practising teachers, of the wide discrepancies exhibited by individuals in empathy for the written word, and responsiveness to early teaching. Many teachers have suggested that during readiness period many children develop adverse attitudes to problem-solving activities and school routines, while others become bored at the protracted exposure to *pre*-reading activities.

Within the last few years, studies of talent and creativity stemming from the work of Guilford (1958), Getzels and Jackson (1962), and Torrance (1960), have already led to revised practices in the U.S.A. of accelerating the talented child, and evidence is available that children are eager and able to profit from pre-school reading experiences (Durkin, 1962), and from earlier admission to school (Barney, 1963). Further questioning of 'readiness' comes from the investigations of the relationship between linguistic skills and intellectual development with the socially disadvantaged child (Reissman, 1962) and the various studies of the cultivation of intellectual growth by means of planned educational stimulation at pre-school level with the educable retarded (Kirk, 1958; Connor and Talbot, 1964) and with the trainable retarded (Lyle and Tizard, 1960; Neale, 1964, 1966, etc.). Elsewhere, in a thoughtful analysis of the educative process, Bruner (1960) has in fact suggested that by carefully evaluating the mode of presentation one might teach almost anything to children of any age. However, despite the growing convergence of opinion, most scientific workers in education share the view of Ausubel (1963) that there is the utmost need for research studies 'showing that learning in a given subject-matter area is more efficient if preceded by a particular kind of other subject matter, . . . and studies showing that more difficult kinds and levels of subject matter—ordinarily not learnable at younger ages—can be learned

Evaluations

successfully if appropriate changes in teaching method are made'. In this respect, then, unstinting tribute must be paid to the British experiment in providing us with the best evidence to date. However, as indicated earlier, scientific inquiry must be extended, while the longitudinal nature of the current research plan will permit a continuing rational reappraisal of theory and practice in the light of emerging data.

i.t.a.—the Medium

Before considering further findings in the i.t.a. investigation it is reasonable to inquire whether the rapid progress of the experimental group can be attributed to the teaching medium, or to other factors such as the increased motivation for learning in teacher and pupils who are the focus of attention in a unique experimental situation. Experience has shown that experimentation, in general, has a boosting effect upon the morale of the group being studied. In the case of i.t.a. it is possible that publicity surrounding the novelty and size of the project, the teacher training sessions and the interim publications have heightened the incentive for reading achievement. The investigator has, however, been aware of this difficulty, and has introduced a number of measures designed to induce similar effects in the control groups. Careful consideration of this point suggests that, even if the investigator's attempts were unsuccessful in producing similar stimulating effects upon the control group, then perhaps other conditions may have had a compensatory effect. Not the least of these would be the professional pride of the control teachers to 'prove' their teaching ability in the use of traditional orthography. Again, the reinforcing quality of everyday stimulation by the printed word in advertisements, television, comics, children's picture books, etc. seems likely to favour the control group. Still further, the availability and range of supplementary reading materials during the teething stage of the experiment seems to have favoured the control group. If we consider also the effect of parent teaching of reading by i.t.a. it seems, to the writer, that the ambivalent feelings of a number of parents to the new medium may have also put the experimental group in a less advantageous position. It seems much more likely that, in ensuing experimentation, the investigators must look to inventive planning to offset the impact of the accumulating favourable publicity of i.t.a.

Turning, therefore, to the Pitman orthography itself, one must consider that the initial teaching alphabet is responsible for the findings. It would appear that i.t.a. permits the young learner to acquire a systematic mode of approach to the problem of discriminating differences in visual patterns. Its few phonic symbols are a less burdensome chore to the immature learner, while the range of the alphabet helps the child to establish a consistent left-to-right orientation in analysing new words. The attempt by Pitman to maintain the general configuration of words of the traditional orthography appears most worthwhile, particularly for easing the process of transfer. Nevertheless, to this writer who has been engaged for many years in diagnostic teaching of dyslexic children, an impartial look at the characters indicates that confusing stimuli still remain. Thus, to the characters p, b, d and g are added ɖh, ʈh, ʃh & ʂh, requiring careful discrimination and memory for fine detail. Without experimental evidence, however, one would not wish to pursue this criticism. Indeed, it could be that the consistency of grapheme-phoneme relationships and the lighter load of phonic symbols assist the learner more swiftly to a higher level of problem-solving wherein he may use contextual clues to aid his guessing of confusing stimuli. Surprisingly too the i.t.a. has been beneficial to those who might be expected to read by any method, enabling them to attain confidence in independent learning. There can be few more ego-building experiences for a child than the objective evidence that he has mastered a new reader alone.

Transfer of Learning

Preliminary accounts of the i.t.a. have frequently produced, in educational circles, comments on the possible adverse effects upon learning when children were transferred to reading in traditional orthography. Particular concern has been expressed for the likelihood that the initial learning would handicap the acquisition of traditional spelling and composition. The evidence to date now indicates that these fears are not supported, since the i.t.a. experimental children show superiority to the control group when assessed in spelling, arithmetic and creative writing. Once again, one must consider the value of the simpler system in providing the learner with a sense of his own effectiveness in structuring the learning process involved in putting words and thoughts on paper.

The success of the experimental children in arithmetic, forces one to the view that the consistency of relationships in i.t.a. induces a positive approach to the search for logical relationships in other phenomena, as in arithmetical problems. The success in traditional spelling appears much more remarkable, but could be related to the initial attentiveness to detail in mastering the recognition and identification of the code. During the ensuing wide range of reading experience, the child is assisted to a new level of maturity of operations. He learns to manipulate the code and translate it to another, much in the manner employed by the individual learning a foreign language.

The larger implications of these three features of the report concern the attitudes of children to literacy skills, particularly in the formative period when failure may have such an inhibiting effect upon the developing personality. In an age when bewildering technological reports and mass media demand not only higher standards of reading ability but habits of critical reading, it would seem that the infant period of education may be critical for the development of such skills. The i.t.a. experiment has demonstrated that infants can acquire perceptual skills rapidly and develop strategies to related learning tasks if the medium of teaching is reasonably simple and consistent in its conventions. Herein is the major contribution of the investigation.

Nevertheless many questions are raised by the study. One of the most interesting, to the writer, would be related to a closer study of the individuals who are in the lowest ten per cent. of the experimental group. It seems that only as one comes to know the difficulties faced by these children can one know how to modify the research design, the timing of transfer to traditional orthography, or the shortcomings of the alphabet itself. There is also an obvious need to document observations of classroom procedures during the transfer period, in order to illuminate those verbal directions which are most effective for developing appropriate expectancies and learning sets. Some intensive studies of the more talented group would also be valuable in understanding the relationship between the learning of i.t.a. and the ability to read for inference, or to supply appropriate words for gaps in the linguistic structure of written material as in some tests of English and intellectual ability.

It is not possible to enumerate, in this brief commentary, the multiplicity of questions which emerge, nor to specify the limitations of the current investigation. At this stage it is important for future progress that the valuable insights obtained from the British experiment be used as a basis for further scientific inquiry into the teaching process.

The i.t.a. *Symposium*

References

AUSUBEL, D. P. (1963). *The Psychology of Meaningful Verbal Learning.* New York: Grune and Stratton.
BARNEY, W. D. (1963). 'The Warren Project on Effectiveness and Feasibility of Early Admission to School of Mentally Advanced Children', *Proceedings of 41st Annual C.E.C. Convention,* Philadelphia, Pennsylvania, 1963.
BRUNER, J. S. (1960). *The Process of Education.* Cambridge, Mass.: Harvard University Press.
BRYANT, N. D. (1964). 'Characteristics of dyslexia and their remedial implication'. *Exceptional Children,* Vol. 31, No. 4, December 1964.
CONNOR, FRANCES, and TALBOT, MABEL E. (1964). *An Experimental Curriculum for Young Mentally Retarded Children* (Teachers College Series in Special Education). New York: Bureau of Publications, Teachers College, Columbia University.
DOWNING, JOHN A. (1962). 'Experiments with an Augmented Alphabet for Beginning Readers in British Schools', presented at the 27th Educational Records Bureau in the City of New York, November 1962.
DOWNING, JOHN A. (1963). 'Experiments with Pitman's Initial Teaching Alphabet in British Schools', presented at the Eighth Annual Conference of the International Reading Association, May 1963.
DOWNING, JOHN A. (1964). *The i.t.a. Reading Experiment.* University of London Institute of Education, Studies in Education.
DOWNING, JOHN A. (   ). *The Initial Teaching Alphabet: A New Two-stage Approach to Learning to Read.* London: Pitman.
DURKIN, DOLORES (1962). 'An earlier start in reading?'. *Elementary School Journal,* 63, December 1962.
FRIEDLANDER, B. (1965). 'A psychologist's second thoughts on concepts, curiosity, and discovery in teaching and learning'. *Harvard Educational Review,* Vol. 35, No. I, Winter 1965.
GANS, ROMA (1963). *Common Sense in Teaching Reading.* New York: Bobbs-Merrill.
GETZELS, J. W. and JACKSON, P. W. (1962). *Creativity and Intelligence.* New York: Wiley.
GRAY, W. S. (1956). *The Teaching of Reading and Writing.* Paris: UNESCO; Chicago: Scott, Foresman.
GUILFORD, J. P. (1959). 'Three faces of intellect'. *Amer. Psychologist,* No. 14, 1959, pp. 469-79.
KEPHART, N. C. (1964). 'Perceptual-motor aspects of learning disabilities'. *Exceptional Children,* Vol. 31, No. 4, December 1964.
KIRK, S. A. (1958). *Early Education for the Mentally Retarded.* Urbana: University of Illinois Press.
KIRK, S. A. (1965). 'Diagnostic, Cultural and Remedial Factors in Mental Retardation', in: *The Biosocial Basis of Mental Retardation,* edited by Sonia F. Osler and Robert E. Cooke.
LYLE, J. G. (1960). 'The effect of an institutional environment upon the verbal development of imbecile children: II, Speech and Language'. *J. Ment. Def. Res.,* Vol. 4, Part I, 1960.
NEALE, M. D. (1964). 'The Effects of a Broad "Art" and "Movement" Programme upon a group of "Trainable" Retarded Children', in: *Proceedings of the International Copenhagen Congress on the Scientific Study of Mental Retardation,* Denmark, 1964.

Evaluations

NEALE, M. D., *et al.* (1966). 'Perceptual development of severely retarded children through motor experience'. *Brit. J. Ment. Sub. Monogr.*, April 1966.

PITMAN, *Sir* JAMES (1961). *Learning to Read*, reprinted from the February 1961 issue of the Journal of the Royal Society of Arts.

REISSMAN, FRANK (1962). *The Culturally Deprived Child.* New York: Harper.

ROBINSON, H. ALAN, ed. (1964). 'Meeting Individual Differences in Reading', *Proceedings of the Annual Conference on Reading held at the University of Chicago*, 1964.

ROBINSON, HELEN M. (1962). 'Summary of investigations relating to reading, 1 July 1960 to 30 June 1961'. *Reading Teacher*, XV, January 1962.

ROBINSON, HELEN M. (1964). 'Developing Critical Reading', *Proceedings of the I.R.A. Oxford Congress on Reading*, 1964.

SMITH, HENRY P. and DECHANT, EMERALD V. (1961). *Psychology in Teaching Reading.* New York: Prentice-Hall.

SUTTON, RACHEL S. (1955). 'A study of certain factors associated with reading readiness in the kindergarten'. *Journal of Educl. Res.*, 48, March 1955, pp. 531-538.

TORRANCE, PAUL (1962). *Guiding Creative Talent.* New York: Prentice-Hall.

VERNON, M. D. (1957). *Backwardness in Reading.* Cambridge: Cambridge University Press.

Evaluations—10

JESSIE F. REID

Department of Education, University of Edinburgh

THERE are a number of inter-related topics which must be kept in mind when this definitive report of the first i.t.a. experiment is assessed. In the compass of a comment of this length, however, it is obviously impossible to discuss every aspect in detail; and a choice must therefore be made.

I shall not discuss the experimental design, except to make one point. Those general principles of randomness in sampling and in allocation of treatment which have not been held to as one would have wished are well set out in Walker and Lev (1953) and in an article by E. G. Shacklock Evans (1962). But, in addition, it detracts greatly from the value of the results that so many different sub-samples have been taken from the initial ones. Under these conditions, statistical inference is of very doubtful validity. I also shall not discuss the 'Hawthorne Effect', except to remark that I do not think the case for its non-existence in this experiment has been proved. All that has been shown is that the efforts made to simulate it were not successful.

I should, however, like to take up in some detail the question of whether 'method' is an uncontrolled variable. From the outset, Downing has maintained that i.t.a. is a 'medium', capable of being used with any method. But the matter is not so simple as this.

In the first place, the word 'method' as used in discussions of the early teaching of reading is often ambiguous. In one sense it covers all the devices which a teacher may employ to interest beginners in print, to enhance their language powers, to make writing and reading meaningful and related to their lives. But in another sense the term is used to refer specifically to the way in which the teaching of the alphabetic code is planned: that is to say, it refers to the Look-and-say approach, to the use of phonics, to vocabulary control and so on. All teachers of infants combine some 'method' in this sense with some of the devices and activities subsumed under the other sense, these providing in many cases the situation or context in which the 'teaching of the code' takes place. But although it is true that i.t.a. *can* be used with any method (in either sense) we have to ask (a) whether this means that method in the second sense is

Evaluations

uninfluenced by it, and (b) whether it ought to be. The first question is one about 'interaction', and could have been answered experimentally if a factorial design had been used and the teachers' methods (in the second sense) classified in some defensible way. But even in the absence of this evidence, we have some clues. Downing remarks (p. 32) that 'a few children seemed to develop phonic analysis and synthesis skills spontaneously'. It was also found by teachers that i.t.a. pupils 'appeared to show readiness for phonics earlier than is usual when t.o. is used'. All teachers of beginning reading want of course to see their pupils arrive finally at the stage when they can 'break the code'. But there are surely many who hold back from encouraging young children to use phonics because they shrink from the prospect of the ensuing confusion and disappointment when the children come up against the words which (to quote a child in an investigation of beginners' difficulties) (Reid, 1958) 'aren't good for sounding' or which have 'not the same letters as you say them in' (Reid, 1966). It is hardly reasonable to doubt that many teachers, no longer faced with exposing children to these frustrations, would take advantage of the opportunity to give them one of the keys to the door of *Janet and John*, Book 1, for instance, presents the following list of words, all containing different sound-values for the letter 'o':

John, come, look, dog, down, one, two, go, horse.

A comparison of i.t.a. and t.o., using a scheme in which special attention is given in the early stages to the control of such anomalies, would seem to be urgently called for.[1]

When one turns to the actual results and tries to look at them in the light of expressed misgivings and current unsolved problems, there is one further thing which should be remembered. It has to do with the meaning of the word 'significant'. Even those who are accustomed to the techniques and the language of statistics have sometimes to remind themselves that the term as applied to (say) an observed difference between two measures means only that this observed amount occurs in the sampling distribution less frequently than some predetermined—and arbitrary—proportion of times, and is therefore being regarded as indicating a 'real' difference in the populations from which the samples were drawn. What the term does *not* mean is that the results are important: a difference could

---

[1] In *In Spite of the Alphabet* (Diack, 1965, p. 175) Diack refers to a piece of unpublished research by Daniels which would appear to bear on this issue.

be hugely 'significant' in statistical terms, and at the same time educationally trivial. In some of the hypotheses set up in this experiment (Nos. 1, 2 and 4 on pp. 3 and 4), the word 'significantly' is used. It appears in the hypotheses without any specification of the level of statistical significance which will be accepted. It is therefore (a) statistically meaningless, and (b) misleading to those who are accustomed to using it in everyday language to mean 'important'.

A study of the tables of results shows that the superiority of the i.t.a. group was not uniform over levels of attainment—a point made by Downing himself. The 'better' i.t.a. children (i.e. those in the top 30 per cent.) gained much more over their t.o. counterparts than did those in the lowest 30 per cent., and this was especially noticeable in the early stages. For many of the poorest, i.t.a. seemed to be of no initial benefit at all, in spite of all the advantages claimed. What must be pointed out, however, is that advantages may have to be taken advantage of. The child learning in i.t.a. who does not spontaneously grasp why recurrences of pattern are there and who is not helped to do so because the material is not primarily designed to emphasize regularities and/or because the teacher is holding grimly to look-and-say approach and not using such opportunities for phonic work as the material provides, has little less—perhaps no less—learning to do than his counterpart learning in t.o. It is at this point that 'clinical' evidence[1] can very fruitfully supplement statistical findings; and my own experiences of interviewing five-year-olds of only moderate ability who were in this very situation supports what has just been argued.

The increasing gains shown by i.t.a. children over t.o. children as the higher levels of achievement are approached could well be the result of their (a) having seen for themselves that the regularities meant something and could be used, and/or (b) having teachers who took full advantage of the possibilities of phonic teaching which i.t.a. inevitably has to offer in any reading scheme.[2] These conjectures are supported by the fact that the area of greatest superiority was 'Accuracy'. The mean difference in Table E3 represents nine months of 'reading age', while the gains represented

---

[1] By this is meant evidence from the interviewing of individual children in a situation which is loosely 'structured', yet free enough to encourage the children to talk about their learning experiences.

[2] I should point out that I am not thinking here of a 'formal phonic approach', which Downing reports finding in only one of the experimental schools.

Evaluations

in E4 and E5 are much less. The educational importance of these differences is of course a separate issue. Those who emphasize 'reading for meaning' might hold that a superiority of four months in Comprehension is as good a sign at this stage as a superiority of nine months in Accuracy.

The justification of i.t.a. in the absence of complete spelling reform must rest entirely on the possibility of transfer, and transfer *for all*—including those, perhaps most of all those—who found reading hard, even in i.t.a. In the part of the report that deals with transfer, the lack of any kind of clinical evidence is again a matter for great regret, for it is only on the basis of such evidence that decisions about fruitful changes in procedure can be taken. The nearest approach to this is the two lists of errors in t.o. words, on Schonell's list and in the Neale passages. But these lists do not report the number of errors made earlier, on the i.t.a. version, by the same children, nor the number made by a corresponding sample of t.o. subjects; nor—most interesting of all—the precise nature of the errors. So the reasons for the errors and the exact nature of them remain matters of pure conjecture, while the relative difficulties found by the two groups can be assessed only by reference to the order in which the words appear in the tests.

The theory of transfer on which the hypotheses are based rests on the assumption (stated on page 18) that the child learns to use visual and semantic redundancy. The tables of errors discussed above, and Downing's comments on pp. 35-38 and pp. 49-51 suggest strongly however that this theory is not adequate to explain success in transfer when it does take place, nor failure when it does not. Many of the successes and failures in reading t.o. words appear not to support it (as Downing himself notes). What may well happen is that children, depending on how they have learned to read initially, bring to the reading of t.o. varying combinations of recognition of similarity (whole or partial), use of context, and learning of *new* phoneme-grapheme relationships, like 'igh' 'ough' and so on, and that no one of these 'bridges' is enough on its own. Further analysis of errors made in isolated words and in words in context would be needed in order to investigate this possibility, and the transfer (or 're-learning') of spelling should be investigated at the same time.

The whole subsequent pattern of slow recovery and final superiority as shown in Tables E16 to E25 is full of potential interest and importance for future decisions about the use of i.t.a.; though this evidence is greatly diminished in value, as I pointed out earlier, by the fact that no two sets of results are on the same samples of children. But taking the figures as they stand, what detailed pattern underlies the overall superiority (a superiority characterized, incidentally, by rather less astronomical significance levels than many of the earlier results) at the end of the third year? The tables in the Statistical Appendix show that although in the lower achievement ranges i.t.a. seems to be associated, for the same reading rate, with considerably higher accuracy and better short-term retention of what had been read, it has not eliminated the 'hard core' of very backward readers. One would very much have liked to know the composition of the bottom ten per cent. who were still achieving very low results. How many were just very poorly endowed or deprived? How many were average or bright? How many were boys? How many at the end of the experiment had not yet transferred successfully at all? The same questions must be asked about the 25 per cent. of i.t.a. children who in mid-fourth year, at an average age of around 8 years 4 months, had spelling ages of 7 years 6 months or less, even although the group as a whole showed some superiority in spelling ability—a finding which has confounded many of the early critics. But, perhaps the most surprising finding comes at the end of the experimental results—namely the figures for the Standish N.S. 45 Test of Silent Reading. Why is it that in this test, after all the earlier superiority, there is no difference between the two groups?

It cannot be ignored that all the previous tests of reading have been oral—the child has heard himself reading, and has been able to solve new words by 'sounding', even though this process may have come to be complex and rapid. Is it possible that when reading has to be silent those children will be at some advantage who, brought up on irregularities, have not had to replace sounding habits by scanning habits to the same extent? Should i.t.a.-taught children perhaps not be transferred until they can read *silently* in i.t.a.? Here is another area where further investigation must be done.

The superiority, as measured by length and variety of vocabulary, of the written work of the i.t.a. group must not be forgotten. It is perhaps one of the most important findings, for it represents an improvement in communicating skill; and it must also have represented real enjoyment for the children. Children will often read to order, but they will write 'stories' only from a desire to record and communicate.

The great need in educational experimentation is for continuity and integration, and we must now ask how the findings of this experiment can be built on. The next step should be to devise and use experimentally material which will, in i.t.a., exploit to the full the regularized and simplified code, and yet in t.o. will maximize opportunities for seeing meaningful similarities. This need not mean a reversion to the artificial and fatuous wording of the 'Dan can fan Nan' variety. That it need not is shown in the ingenious system of Richards and Gibson, working with the maximum of regularity in t.o. and with a restricted alphabet. It is also shown in the work of Daniels and Diack. Along with this exploitation of the code, however, should go radical re-thinking about the content of infant primers, not in the sense of 'themes'—though these need some scrutiny too—but in the sense of linguistic structure.

There have been numerous studies of the vocabularies of young children, and these have been used as source books for the construction of reading primers. But so far, there seems to have been no systematic study of the sentence structures used by five-year-olds with a view to making similar use of these. Yet the theory which claims that only words familiar to the child should be used in the earliest books he encounters—that is, that the teaching of code-breaking should not be confounded with the teaching of new vocabulary—ought to extend to syntax as well. It has been demonstrated (Reid, 1958) that a child can recognize a word in one context, and a few moments later meet the same word in a less familiar linguistic setting and assert that he has never seen it before and does not know it. For instance, he may be able to read: 'We went back to the deep mud' and 'You must give me more words to read'; yet be unable to read: 'You must not go back on your word' or 'We must not give up when work is hard'. These methods which already make use of children's own dictated sentences as first reading material may well owe their success not only to high motivation, content interest, and so on, but to the fact that the sentence structures and the idioms are inevitably within the child's linguistic competence. The time has now come, however, when the techniques of linguistic analysis ought to make it possible to differentiate and describe the types of syntactic structure which five-year-olds will find most familiar and natural.

It could well be that in combination with the other kinds of control I have indicated, i.t.a.—perhaps in a somewhat modified form—will prove to have a permanent part to play in the teaching of reading. But we need much more breakdown of its effects at different stages and with different kinds of children; we need to study the interaction of medium with method and material; we need clinical study of the complex and little understood phenomena of transfer; and we need to know the result of the quiet integration of the best features of the system into ordinary classroom practice.

References

DANIELS, J. C. and DIACK, HUNTER (1954). *The Royal Road Readers*. London: Chatto and Windus.
DIACK, HUNTER (1965). *In Spite of the Alphabet*. London: Chatto and Windus.
DOWNING, J. A. (1965). 'The initial teaching alphabet'. *New Society*, 11th February, 1965.
EVANS, E. G. SHACKLOCK (1962). 'The design of teaching experiments in education'. *Educational Research*, Vol. V, No. 1, 37-52.
REID, JESSIE F. (1958). 'An investigation of thirteen beginners in reading'. *Acta Psychologica*, Vol. XIV, No. 4, 295-313.
REID, JESSIE F. (1966). 'Learning to think about reading'. *Educational Research*. Vol. 9, No. 1, pp. 56-62.
RICHARDS, I. A. and GIBSON, CHRISTINE (1943). *Words on Paper. First Steps in Reading*. Cambridge, Mass.: English Language Research.
WALKER, HELEN and LEV, JOSEPH (1953). *Statistical Inference*. New York: Holt.

Evaluations—11

M. D. VERNON
Professor of Psychology, University of Reading

THE most important finding of Downing's report is constituted by the results on the Neale Test of Reading Ability (printed in t.o.) of the 800 and more children who began three years earlier to learn to read by i.t.a., compared with those of their matched controls who had used t.o. throughout. At this time, the i.t.a. group showed a significant superiority over the t.o. group of about 5 months in reading age, on the average, in accuracy, speed and comprehension on the Neale test. There was no significant difference between the two groups on the Standish N.S. 45 test. But this is a group test of reading, and the results were probably less reliable, for the distribution of scores (see the Statistical Appendix) was markedly irregular.

The average superiority of the i.t.a. group at this point is all the more notable in that about six months earlier there was little significant difference between the two groups. During the early period, while they were reading only i.t.a., the experimental group had forged well ahead. But clearly they experienced considerable difficulty in transferring from i.t.a. to t.o.; and even those who had had six weeks practice with t.o. obtained lower scores on the Neale test printed in t.o. than they had gained previously on the Neale test printed in i.t.a. It would appear that they were still confused by the irregular spelling of many t.o. words. But it is possible that the teachers, who were relatively unskilled in handling the transfer, might be able to improve in this respect in future.

It would seem also that the i.t.a. children were superior, after transfer, to the t.o. children in both spelling and writing, although the method by which written compositions were assessed was not very satisfactory. It is understandable that the children should have been able to write more easily and fluently in i.t.a. before transfer; but it would be a great advantage of the i.t.a. if the superiority were permanently maintained afterwards.

Downing therefore appears to be justified in claiming the superiority of i.t.a. over t.o. *in the circumstances in which he carried out his investigation.* To what extent this finding can be generalized is more doubtful. It seems from his very clear description of the manner in which the investigation was performed that the situation for the i.t.a. group was essentially 'experimental'. Preparations were hurried, and there were difficulties in arranging the inquiry and in providing the necessary i.t.a. reading books. The i.t.a. teachers may have been impeded by these conditions, and anxious as to their ability to work with the new medium. On the other hand, they may have been stimulated to extra effort by the sense of emergency, the novelty of the situation, the special training they received, Downing's frequent visits to them and the general publicity accorded to the investigation. The children may have been stimulated by encouragement from their parents, who were sent a special circular describing the i.t.a. Though some parents felt misgivings, others may have been flattered by the special attention their children were receiving. It is impossible to decide whether these factors were, on balance, favourable or unfavourable to the teaching of the i.t.a., or had no effect.[1] But quite clearly the whole situation was extremely different from that found in the relatively stable and unvarying conditions in which children normally learn to read, and it is risky to predict from what occurred in the former situation what could happen in the latter. It is true that Downing found no such effects with the t.o. group, which showed much the same achievement in reading as that of children in the same schools who began learning to read a year before the commencement of the experiment. But this finding has no relevance to the i.t.a. group.

It is unfortunate that, presumably for the sake of administrative convenience, the i.t.a. and the t.o. classes were drawn from different schools.[2] Moreover, the children were matched individually, and not the school classes. This procedure inevitably introduced the factor of inter-school variability. And it appeared from the results obtained for the t.o. schools in the pre-research period that the average reading performance varied very greatly between schools; and similar results have been discovered by other investigators.

---

[1] The number and complexity of such factors, and those described in the following paragraph, are demonstrated in a recent article by J. D. WILLIAMS ('Some problems involved in the experimental comparison of teaching methods'. *Educational Research*, 1965, 8, 26-41), who discusses them in greater detail than is possible here in connection with an investigation into the comparative efficiency of traditional and modern methods of teaching arithmetic. His inquiry poses problems very similar to those encountered in the introduction of i.t.a.

[2] In a more recent study by DOWNING and JONES ('Some problems of evaluating i.t.a.—a second experiment'. *Educational Research*, 1966, 8, 100-14), i.t.a. and t.o. classes were drawn from the same schools and taught by the same teachers. But here other difficulties arose in comparing the effects of the two media.

Evaluations

Downing controlled his results for differences in certain physical features such as urban or rural situation, size of school, amenities, etc., and also for the social class of the children's fathers. But he did not control for variation between schools in method and adequacy of teaching and the time given to teaching reading; nor for such important but intangible factors as the general morale and progressiveness, or otherwise, of the schools. A study of the reading performance in the i.t.a. schools in the pre-research period could presumably have indicated whether they also normally showed wide variations in reading achievement, and whether they were in general similar to, better or worse than the t.o. schools. Probably some kind of analysis of variance of the results would be necessary to establish the significance and inter-relation of all the above factors and their effect on reading achievement. Downing himself states in the Statistical Appendix that a multivariate analysis of the results would have been desirable, but that it was not possible to carry out the appropriate techniques. Nevertheless, that the results of investigations such as this may differ in differing situations is indicated by a small-scale but well controlled study by Swales,[1] in which it was found that after three years of learning reading, children who began with the i.t.a. showed no significant superiority over those who had learnt t.o. throughout.

We must now consider the general importance of the contribution made by the i.t.a. to the learning of reading, supposing Downing's results to be substantiated by further experiment. Who really benefited by the i.t.a. and in what way? Downing attempted to discover the extent to which learning occurred in children showing different degrees of reading ability. He presents, somewhat cursorily, graphs of test scores for successive decile groups of attainment. From those at the third year of learning reading it appears that children of greater ability derived relatively more benefit from i.t.a. than did children of less ability. However, the former would probably learn to read with little difficulty whatever the medium used. The i.t.a. would be of far greater value to education if it helped the poorer performers and produced a decrease in the number of backward readers. But if one studies the data given in Tables 27 and 29 of the Statistical Appendix (showing the frequencies of different scores on the Neale test at the third year) one finds that in the i.t.a.

---

[1] SWALES, T. D. (1966). 'The attainments in reading and spelling of children who learned to read through the initial teaching alphabet'. Unpublished M.Ed. Thesis, University of Manchester, 1966.

group 9.8 per cent. obtained ten marks or less for accuracy and 13.9 per cent. obtained five marks or less for comprehension (in both cases these marks correspond to reading ages of under seven years). The corresponding frequencies for the t.o. group were 17.5 per cent. and 24.7 per cent. respectively. Thus it would seem that, contrary to Downing's conclusion, there *were* fewer children of poor reading ability in the i.t.a. than in the t.o. group. However, the Neale test is not very satisfactory at low levels of achievement; and the number of severely backward readers is too small to enable any conclusions to be drawn. One might surmise that the less able would benefit relatively more at the early stages while learning the regular orthography of the i.t.a.; but might find the transition from this to the irregularities of t.o. particularly difficult to perform. Further investigation of this hypothesis is needed.

Downing bases his plea for the general adoption of the i.t.a. on the argument that children learning t.o. are forced to undergo unnecessary difficulties in learning to read by the lack of clear and regular correspondence between letter shapes and sounds. Obviously the children must of necessity surmount this difficulty sooner or later. But it is arguable that they are better able to do so at the age at which they transfer from i.t.a. to t.o., when they are more mature, than as beginners. However, it is possible that a later beginning of formal reading teaching, and a phonic method which only gradually introduces anomalies of grapheme-phoneme correspondence, might be almost as effective in eliminating this difficulty as learning the regular i.t.a. correspondence between graphemes and phonemes and then unlearning it in many cases when transfer takes place. And none of these procedures seems guaranteed to overcome what often seems to be the principal difficulty: that the child, knowing how to sound printed letters and graphemes, cannot combine these sounds into total sound patterns which match the sound patterns of words as he commonly pronounces them. This failure to perform a process of synthesis which demands considerable skill in abstraction and generalization is well known in severely backward readers; and it may also create a stumbling block for other beginners in reading. It would seem that the failure could be largely prevented by using more modern phonic methods of teaching in which phonemes are always presented in whole words, and thus analysis is immediately followed by re-synthesis.

Downing himself states that much further study is required to elucidate the many problems which have arisen in the course of his investigation. To the writer, it would seem essential to perform

Evaluations

an intensive long-term study on a relatively small number of children to determine exactly what are the major points of difficulty in learning to read, both when t.o. is used throughout, and also when transfer is made to t.o. from earlier i.t.a. teaching. This should culminate in a comparison of the ultimate ability developed in the two conditions to read fluently for comprehension. In the meanwhile, one must conclude that it is excessively difficult to prove the value of any reform in educational method and congratulate Downing on his first attempt.

The Evaluations: A Summary

by

W. D. WALL

The Evaluations: a Summary

W. D. WALL,

National Foundation for Educational Research in England and Wales

IN attempting to evaluate this research report and the contributions of the symposiasts, we must remind ourselves of two things. First, Downing was essentially concerned with two closely related questions: is the irregularity of English orthography a serious cause of difficulty to children learning to read in infant and junior schools? And does the Initial Teaching Alphabet simplify the process in a significant way? Other questions arise out of these and many problems occurred along the way, but these should not obscure the points at issue. The second thing of which we should remind ourselves, is that the i.t.a. inquiry is a field action study, the first of its kind and scale reported in the United Kingdom. Not surprisingly, many of its difficulties and imperfections became apparent only to hindsight. It is possible that answers to the specific problems posed or to others which have been put would have been more easily obtained and more surely established had the research team adopted an entirely different approach. This is something which I personally doubt, in common with many of the contributors to this book. In matters of the present kind, the field study is ultimately always necessary, if only to test the ideal against the real.

A field trial of the present kind has certain very great advantages. It takes as its starting point, teachers, classes, schools and children as they are in the day to day business of education rather than an ideal or laboratory situation. Anything certainly established in these circumstances is likely to be readily generalizable and establishes —as Burt points out—a *prima facie* case. However, the field study introduces difficulties of its own, and if the methods imposed by it are seriously criticizable, then the results, however apparently clear, must be regarded with suspicion. Most of the contributors have been quick to point out various defects. The first of these is the difficulty of controlling the interfering or 'nuisance' variables— differences between schools, differences in the motivation, enthusiasm and skill of the teachers, differences due to the way that controversy sharpened and made highly emotional the issues involved, often obscuring what were the real questions.

The Evaluations: a Summary

Such features are, in fact, part of the reality of school life and will always be so particularly when innovations are advocated and meet with the anxious conservatism of parents and part of the teaching profession. To have avoided such circumstances might have improved the rigour of the design: it would not, however, have made a field trial unnecessary. One should ask whether all was done that could be to minimize the effects of such possible nuisance variables —and particularly the Hawthorne Effect. Most of the contributors pay a well deserved tribute to Downing for his attempt to control these variables as far as possible and applaud the caution with which he presents his results. Certain criticisms are, however, sustained and do limit the generalizability of the results. There was and could not be any real randomness of sampling of schools and teachers: by and large these were self-selected. However, the numbers of them—and especially of teachers—would to some (unknown) extent tend to reduce bias and a real effort was made to organize the same kind of enthusiasm and stimulus in the control schools as in the experimental ones. It is further worth remarking that we know very little about the alleged Hawthorne Effect (which arises as a concept from a study of *adult workers*) in terms of five to seven year old children and their teachers. *A priori* reasoning would suggest that it is probably very different and, since the first years of school are, for most children, a period of heightened emotionality anyway, it *may* be negligible.

Much more serious is the fact that for easily understandable reasons, the principal analyses are based upon the child as a unit. Much research has told us that inter-school and inter-class variability is considerable and that, in work of the present kind, the main unit for sampling and analysis should probably be the class. This point is made by Holmes and in different ways by Reid, Burt and Vernon.

Some, but not all of the analyses are by school or class, though matching was not and could not be rigorous; much of the evidence rests upon inter-child comparisons and can take no note of inter-school and inter-class variability. A factorial design would have been less open to criticism; but its exigencies would have clashed with those imposed by the voluntary nature of participation.

Admitting that this is experimentally and statistically a defect (but that, in field studies of the present kind, it is sometimes inevitable) is it so serious as to invalidate the results completely? The majority of the contributors concur to reply 'no'. The results put forward by Downing are coherent: and since they hang together with remarkable consistency, the probability seems to be that any defects in design have reduced the clearcutness of the conclusions and limited rather than undermined their validity. Generalization may be made with caution.

But what generalizations may we in fact make? Young children provided with a medium (*not a method*) which removes some at least of the irregularities of English orthography and thus simplifies the stimulus at the initial stages of learning to read, do master certain aspects of reading faster than they appear to do under the normal conditions. We are justified in concluding that the irregularity of English spelling is a cause of difficulty in learning to read for children between the ages of five and seven. It is, too, justifiable to add that i.t.a. itself simplifies the learning task significantly. Diack, of course, points out that simplification is possible within the ordinary orthography and alphabet, if the teacher is prepared to exploit such regularity as exists already in English and suggests that all that has been proved is that alphabetic approaches to reading through phonically graded material may be better than others. Though this begs most of the important questions, it betrays a left-handed kind of agreement. In any case, a much wider vocabulary with regular grapheme-phoneme correspondence is available in i.t.a. than could be with the current alphabet and spelling.

Within this generally favourable conclusion, there are some cautions raised. The first is that the superiority of the experimental groups is not uniform. The better thirty per cent of children—who in any case would learn well and fast—gain more than do the less able thirty per cent. One would hope—though the hope is rarely justified in practice—that simplification would benefit those who have most difficulty. Gulliford, however, points out two things: first, that while it is true that after two and a half years, there are still about fifteen per cent of the i.t.a. taught children on Books 1 and 2, there are fewer than in the control groups; secondly—a point made in a different way by Burt—that the causes of reading failure are known in many, even in most, cases to be independent of any method or medium of teaching. They reside in the child, in his prior experience, his level of maturity, his attitudes and so on. A number of contributors point out that the inquiry did not seek to exploit the possibilities of i.t.a. in relation to method, but left teachers free to use it as they saw best. That this was so would, of course, tend to diminish any overall superiority and might particularly affect the least able. Burt suggests that the medium itself is more suitable for pupils who are predominantly audile and motile in their approach to reading and less so for the visualizers and for the dull. Hemming

The Evaluations: a Summary

stresses that the results suggest very strongly that a modification in the methods used in the early stages, exploiting the use of phonic cues made possible by regularization of orthography, is essential.

Some of the writers look at this point in another way—notably Hemming and Gulliford. A regularized orthography makes certain things more possible and easier to do; it does not bring them about. Gulliford points out that the results are entirely consistent with this strictly facilitating effect—it is, for example, the lower order decoding skills (word recognition) which are most improved and any effects on higher order skills, comprehension for example, are not so clear. There is, as several point out, some evidence of superiority in written work, and some apparent spread to school work generally. In the light of what we know of the educational process, especially the learning of young children, one would expect many factors to contribute the different rates of progress—the child's own maturity and conceptual level, the skill with which home and teacher arouse his enthusiasm to learn—among which the facilitation of initial learning, and early sensation of progress would be important but by no means a unique spur. What seems surprising and encouraging to the present writer is just that the indirect effects, on comprehension, on free writing and on general morale did in fact occur and are, in general, rather on the side of the i.t.a. taught children. It is difficult to think that this could be solely or even principally due to the supposed Hawthorne Effect; it seems at least likely to be a product of one or both of two things: either the earlier start made, particularly by the brighter children, speeded up (by making them possible) the wider aspects of intellectual growth which come with independent reading; or, because teachers were able to give less attention to the formal aspects, they could give more time to encouraging and guiding children's general verbal and creative development.

One thing it certainly does suggest is that conventional notions of readiness, particularly in their rather over-simplified and rigid forms, already under attack from other evidence, now need, as Neale points out, very substantial revision. Here we stumble upon a point made, particularly by Vernon, but implicit in other contributions and which certainly underlay much of the opposition to the experiment. Many experts concerned with the education of young children deprecate an early start on the formal learning of reading. Vernon suggests that if the teaching of reading is put off altogether until the first junior school years, children would, because of their generally greater maturity, be able to cope with the ordinary orthography with much less difficulty. Nothing in the present experiment proves or disproves this; the critical experiments have yet to be made, though it does seem to be generally true that a slower start does not necessarily imply a lower level of attainment at, say, eleven or thirteen. Against this, it must also be said that—again much of the evidence is cited by Neale—deprived children seem to profit from deliberately planned systematic educational stimulation as early as possible in their lives, even in the pre-school period. An early mastery of reading might well open up areas of experience, possibilities of conceptual growth and of linguistic development which would hold out some hope of making more real the notion of educational equality. In the present study there is nothing to contradict such a hope: there is indeed much to encourage it.

Of course, were the problems of transition to conventional orthography to prove serious and insurmountable, then we should be back where we were. In evaluating the evidence on this point, we must bear in mind that a new medium is bound to raise new problems—as Morgan and Procter are quick to suggest. No attempt was made to assist teachers in developing particular strategies to smooth the transition; nor was guidance given as to when the transition should be made. One would expect, therefore, that any set-back would be the more serious. It is, in fact, much less than one might reasonably fear and curiously enough does not seem to affect spelling—rather the reverse. The less able children have the most difficulty and all children seem to suffer a check. The worst that can be said—on the evidence of the group test of silent reading—is that the i.t.a. children *seem* to have gained a little. In fact the position is much better than this since, over all the measures used including orally administered tests (which are generally more reliable than group tests at the ages concerned) and the book criterion, the balance is in favour of the i.t.a. children, particularly in the lower order decoding skills which form the foundation of subsequent progress. Full confirmation of this can only come from further follow-through studies of the two groups.

It is, however, quite clear—and Downing himself is at great pains to emphasize this—that i.t.a. is neither perfect in itself as a medium of simplification nor is it (or any more refined medium of a similar kind) a panacea. The processes by which children learn to read, learn to love and use reading as an important intellectual and emotional tool in their own growth are highly complex. A medium or even a method touches only part of the process: it is the skill, knowledge and insight of the teacher which alone will enable him to take advantage of whatever technology he may have at his dis-

The Evaluations: a Summary

posal in helping each individual child to profit from the opportunities the school offers. In my view, Downing has been unfairly criticized for not examining and bringing into his field experiment all these other aspects of method and teaching skill. This would be appropriate to a very large team with a broad brief to investigate all phases of reading over a long period of time. This, however, he was not charged or financed to do. In fact, in material available to the symposiasts, but not published in this volume, he has dealt with some of the points raised, notably those concerned with the analysis of perceptual processes.

Research is open-ended and tends to raise more questions than it settles. A principal one hangs over i.t.a. itself. Inevitably it is somewhat *ad hoc;* and it is clear from the report itself and from many of the contributions, notably those of Artley, Holmes, Morgan and Procter and Neale, that the medium itself—now that the idea has been shown to be worthy of attention—should be very closely examined, in the context of individual studies of children's learning and, as Reid puts it, of a radical rethinking of children's primers in the sense of their linguistic structure. Other contributors insist on the need for method studies in which teachers are helped to exploit to the full the possibilities inherent in a simplified medium and in which groups of children are followed through, with controls from the same schools, over a number of years. Yet others, and notably Morgan and Procter, point to the need to study the problems with which a new medium confronts the teacher, to provide some training in the use of it, including a warning of the possibility of spontaneous variation, and of the danger inherent in assuming that the medium itself is a substitute for a teacher's own thoughtful intervention in the learning and transfer processes.

It is not without significance that of the eleven contributors, nine should have thus emphasized the need for further research to develop the present work along a variety of lines, most of them concerned in one way or another with the interaction between an improved simplified code, the child's own learning processes and the nature of the teacher's intervention. In his introduction to the present book, Elvin raises the point that the way in which this inquiry was launched, the mode of its finances (and it should be added here, the doubt which hangs over the future of the Unit itself) precluded and precludes the overall sustained and planned attack on the problems of learning to read which are certainly warranted. Without substantial private and foundation funds, the work of the Reading Research Unit would never have started; if more money had been

The i.t.a. *Symposium*

available, some at least of the gaps could have been filled and some of the defects in the research design been improved, if not removed. If the work is to be exploited, as it should be, and particularly if we are to avoid the adoption of the present half-way house as the best that can be done, considerable support for further work on reading will be required after 1 May 1967.

One final thing should be said and, in terms of the development of the technologies of education, it is perhaps the most important. In this country educational research has, in general, been on too small a scale to be fully-effective; such large-scale studies as we have had, probing into the living realities of the schools, have tended to be operational, exploring and assessing the varieties of an already existing situation. For the most part, innovations have escaped objective study and, if evaluated at all, have been assessed mainly on partisan opinion. Faith rather than science has been the guide. In the phase into which education seems now to be passing of large-scale innovation in method, curriculum and organization, there are not wanting many and powerful voices to say that objective evaluation is unnecessary or impossible. The work carried out by Downing and his team gives the lie to both.